PROJECT MANAGEMENT FOR ENVIRONMENTAL SAFETY & HEALTH PROFESSIONALS

18 Steps to Success

F. David Pierce

Government Institutes, Inc.
Rockville, MD

Government Institutes, Inc., 4 Research Place, Rockville, Maryland 20850, USA.

Library of Congress Cataloging-in-Publication Data

Pierce, F. David.
    Project management for environmental, safety and health professionals / by F. David Pierce.
        p.   cm.
    Includes bibliographical references and index.
    ISBN: 0-86587-598-7
    1. Industrial safety--Management 2. Industrial project management.
I. Title.
   T55.P525   1997
   658.4 '04--dc21
                                   97-37709
                                   CIP

PROJECT MANAGEMENT FOR ENVIRONMENTAL, SAFETY AND HEALTH PROFESSIONALS

CONTENTS

iii

DEDICATION

To all entrepreneurs who have chased dreams that lie deep inside, whether or not they were visible or understood by others around them. To those who dance to an inner drum that says, "I know I can," even against extreme odds, negative talk, harsh treatment, and worse. To those who, successful in realizing their dreams or not, know that merely having those dreams and the adventure of chasing them is reward and acknowledgement. You are special, courageous people. You are true paradigm pioneers.

PREFACE

In life, everything tends to run together. Like a watercolor painting left wet, everything tends to blend into one indescribable color and image. This is the way it often is in our working lives—everything tends to blend together. Every task and project is done in the same way, using the same skills, and keeping to the same schedule. Working on a sampling plan, a new ventilation system, a compliance program for a new standard, or an accident investigation—all tasks blend together into the canvas of our workday. Get one task done...then move on to the next.

Wait a minute! Shouldn't different tasks require different skills, different methods, and different approaches? If we stop and think about it, well....yes, of course they should. But that isn't the way we view them in real life, at the time we are completing them. Instead, all tasks tend to blend together, one after the next.

But most of us see projects very differently. Projects are different from the routine. Projects require special skills and special attention. Their nature and impact are different. The criticality of completing a project is different from that of completing a routine task. The visibility of projects to upper management is different. For all of these reasons, projects simply cannot be handled in the same way and with the same skills as routine tasks. Projects require special skills and attention.

Unfortunately, we tend to learn this reality only after a project blows up in our faces. That's a pity. Because of a project's critical nature and visibility, after a project fails is a poor time to learn lessons like this. But the truth is, too often we in the environmental, safety, and health arena learn project management only through trial and error.

Project management requires special skills and attention to specific aspects of our organizational world and our jobs. We often miss this fact. We also miss the reality that all these skills and attention are learned, just like the specialty skills we master on a daily basis. We learn our specialty, whether it be safety, industrial hygiene, environmental, or other, and having done that, we assume that we have all the necessary skills to be successful. But then along comes a simple project and we struggle to fit our learned skills to that new area.

Like most people, the difference between project management skills and other specialty skills escaped me. I really didn't think about or worry about my project management abilities. Projects would go on all around me. Some would be successful and others would flop—thinking back, most struggled. But I wasn't tuned in to what was really going on.

For example, once I was helping a company to understand why their safety and environmental department wasn't working effectively. Before I was scheduled to meet with department personnel, I began to arrive early and talk to the secretaries. As with most organizations, if you really want to know what's going on, ask the secretaries. The department was heavily focused on projects—projects of all kinds. They were coordinating this project here, planning that one over there, fixing the problems in another one. Their list of projects grew monthly but none of them ever seemed to fall off the list. None of them ever seemed to be completed.

I came to two opposing questions: "Why aren't our projects being completed?" and "What advantage is there to us if the project list just continues to grow?" The answer to the second question is obvious, and a common one. The issue of "turf" stalled most of the projects. In other words, a heavy list of projects, whether backlogged or in progress, was insurance that the manpower and budget would be secured.

That brought me back to the first question of why projects were not being completed. This answer, too, was obvious after talking to several of the project managers. Everyone did projects differently. Some projects worked, most didn't, but there was no commonality or common language to project management. Nonstandardized practices not only destroyed progress, they made communication and coordination between the many methods and techniques impossible to manage. It was a mess. At that moment, I began to understand how important project management skills—and the standardization of those skills—was to an organization. These skills were different than any other skills. They were critical and unique.

After practicing in the field of environmental safety and health for over twenty-five years, an overwhelming reality struck me—we don't have any formal or informal education on how to effectively manage projects. What a miscalculation! If projects receive designated budgets, have inflated expectations, have unrealistic time expectations, and are visible to upper management, why shouldn't we take the time to learn the skills necessary to do them successfully? I'll openly admit that after seeing all the blunders we've made in trying to manage projects, I still have no perfect answer for that question.

This book was written to bridge the gap in our knowledge that exists between current skills and effective project management skills. Effective project management is really just a new learned skill. It doesn't arise from black magic, luck, or anything else. It is simply an application of learnable project management skills. This book discusses the truths about how we traditionally manage projects and, therefore, have failed. It provides insight into how we must approach project management with a method that can be used to successfully manage projects 100 percent of the time. This is not an idle boast. Project management is the practice of a learned skill. Given the knowledge and a method that works, project management is something that all of us can do effectively and successfully *every time* we are handed the ball. With these skills, you can say with confidence, "I'm ready, Coach, just give me the ball."

PROJECT MANAGEMENT FOR ENVIRONMENTAL SAFETY & HEALTH PROFESSIONALS

1

INTRODUCTION: SKILLS FOR SUCCESS

A veteran environmental, safety and health professional joined a consulting firm after working twenty years in industry. His hiring was envisioned as a real step-up in the firm's experience repertoire. Immediately, the advantages of the firm's wise hiring decision were evident in the number of new clients who started returning cold calls and solicitations. "Best decision I ever made," the firm's executive openly said. With projected sales increasing by 30 percent, indeed, this decision looked like a real winner.

The first major job the new consultant was named to lead was a complex project for a large chemical facility that included environmental, safety and health aspects. None of the steps were terribly difficult but required some detailed planning and intricate implementation. The new consultant had excellent communication and interpersonal skills to bank on. The discovery meetings at the beginning of the project were very fruitful and received open accolades from the customer. Planning was complex, as expected. It required extensive communication and coordination of different resources, subcontractors, and customer personnel. In fact, the planning became so complex, suddenly it seemed that only the new consultant knew what was going on, when it would happen, and who needed to be involved. Needless to say, this made the customer a little worried. The project was important and the time demands stringent, but the customer also wanted to know how the project was progressing.

Work began on schedule but quickly fell behind. Resources that were needed didn't show up on time. Other resources or communications were hurriedly added and then deleted from the schedule. The agreed upon milestones were being missed. The new consultant began to spend extra hours at the chemical facility to handle the day-to-day, minute-to-minute coordination and communication. The first warning flag appeared when the consulting company billed for excessive hours that were being charged to the project. Overbillings also began to be received from subcontractors.

"How's the project coming?" The consulting company's executive queried after seeing the preliminary accounting sheets. "It's tight. There are a lot of unanticipated, unrecognized things happening. But, we still have plenty of wiggle room," the new consultant offered.

The project went from 8-hour to 16-hour workdays. Weekend work came next. When the third request for cost overruns hit the customer's management, the questions became harder, faster, and more urgent. The project seemed to be hopelessly behind schedule and expensive. A formal request would have to be made to the regulatory agencies for extensions. These would come with new consulting charges and probably fines from the agencies. Who would bear these additional costs? Needless to say, relations between the customer and the consulting company became strained.

An oversight consultant was hired to come in and look over the project and, if necessary, take a managing role. The project was a mess. It was 2.5 times over budget and three months behind schedule. That's when the worst happened. At 6:15 a.m. one morning, a large earthmover backed over and killed a subcontractor employee. The operator of the earthmover was completing his 18th straight hour on the job. There was so much activity in the area where the man was killed that no one could hear the earthmover's back-up alarm. The preliminary accident investigation discovered that it was questionable whether anyone would have listened to the alarm even if they could hear it because of the hectic activity in the area.

The company, the consultant, the involved contractors, and the regulatory agencies stopped the project immediately for a full investigation. The findings were long and ugly. As a result, the consulting contract was canceled. The family of the killed worker filed a lawsuit against the consulting firm and the chemical company. The chemical company also filed suit to reclaim some of the financial losses it suffered and would continue to suffer. The whole project was a disaster. What went wrong? Why did it have such a disastrous end? What could be learned to prevent this from happening again?

ASSUMPTIONS

Assuming things seems to be a human fingerprint. We assume things all the time. We assume others know things that they don't. We assume that something will happen, but then it doesn't. We assume that skills exist when they don't. We assume someone will handle something, but then they don't. Assuming seems to be a sure-fired path to failure but we continue on, making assumptions all the time without learning. Assuming things seems to be a fatal flaw of the human animal.

What kinds of assumptions were made that contributed to this example of a consulting disaster? There were assumptions made everywhere. The consulting company that hired the twenty-year professional assumed that he had the skills necessary for the practice of consulting. Further, they assumed that he was skilled in project management when they assigned him to the chemical facility's project. The new consultant assumed that successful project management was merely an extension of the other skills he had acquired over his twenty years. The chemical company assumed that the consulting firm had the necessary skills for managing a complex and important project. The consulting firm's executive assumed—even when the numbers said differently—that the new consultant had control of the project. The chemical firm assumed that everything would be okay, even as project overruns kept coming in the door. There were faulty assumptions everywhere and by everyone.

PROJECT MANAGEMENT AS A LEARNED SKILL

"What do you want to be when you grow up?" When we were young, we fully recognized that learning was a necessary step to being who or what we wanted to be. If we wanted to be policemen, we needed to become skilled at police activities including shooting, self-defense, law, etc. If we wanted to be physicians, we recognized that we had to go to school to learn the necessary skills. It's the same anytime we take on new responsibilities or try new professional paths. We must first develop the skills necessary to be successful. Make no mistake about it. Effectively managing a project is a skill not a talent. For that matter, it is not a natural outgrowth of the practice or schooling in safety, health, industrial hygiene, environment, or management. It is instead a specialized skill that one must acquire if he or she is to be successful at managing projects.

Before we jump to the assumption that project management skills are only necessary for consultants and not us, we need to look at how projects impact our jobs. When you really think about it, projects make up a significant part of all our jobs. Whether the project you're leading is improving a ventilation system, starting a new safety awareness campaign, changing management concepts, starting up a hazmat team, writing a safety manual, developing a compliance program for a major standard or change in regulations, improving or starting your contractor safety program, evaluating exposures on a new production line, implementing a safety program at a new construction site, selecting and purchasing new safety or environmental technology, writing and submitting an environmental permit application, negotiating a settlement of a regulatory citation or notice of violation, you will always be dealing with projects during your employment. Each project is unique and comes with its own challenges and time demands. Projects are never "cookie cutter" issues where you simply do the same thing again or do something the same way you did something else. Each project is unique and, therefore, so is its management.

WHY ARE PROJECT MANAGEMENT SKILLS SO IMPORTANT?

When I was young, I watched my parents drive while I was a passenger in the car. "What's so tough about that?" I wondered. I mean, you simply sat in the left front seat of the car, worked some pedals on the floor, played with a gearshift when the engine noise got loud, and steered the car where you wanted it to go. Anyone could drive a car, right? It seemed pretty easy from observation. But do you remember the first time you sat behind the wheel for your first solo experience? Chances are that it was not a relaxed picture. Gripping the steering wheel with enough force to crush small animals, our minds were full of all that we had to remember. "Let me see...clutch in all the way, then put the car in first gear, bring up the RPMs with the right foot and gradually let up on the clutch until the RPMs start to drop, add a little more push on the accelerator, continue to release the clutch, and viola, movement!" Easy, right? Was it really as simple as it seemed from observation? "Too much gas. Too little gas. Too fast letting the clutch out. Too slow. Wrong gear! Killed it again!" It wasn't as easy as it looked! Driving a car took some practice and learning of skills to perfect.

So, we invested the time to learn and perfect the skill of driving. Why? Because driving was cool! I mean, it is so cool to drive through the parking lot at school with your left arm resting on the windowsill, a little slouched back in the seat. Man, that's cool. If we were required to learn how to drive and saw no advantage in it, I really doubt if many of us would have invested the time and effort. One frustrating ride would be quite enough of an experience to determine that this skill was for someone else.

Actually, with the amount of driving that we do (some much more than others) in our lives, it's a pretty good thing that driving was cool and we developed the skill. Driving is a skill most of us use all the time. Driving is a significant part of our lives, and, in a lot of cases, part of our jobs. This is my point about project management skills—if it's a significant part of our jobs, and, for that matter, our lives, shouldn't we have the skills to do it well?

The normal assumption here can lead us to disaster just as it did the new consultant who joined the consulting company after twenty years of practice in his profession. We can assume that project management is simply no big deal. After all, if we can effectively manage a checkbook and know when to come in from the rain, project management skills are obviously easy and natural, aren't they? Just like that young passenger in the car who assumes that driving is simple, we can make the same assumption of project management.

The assumptions we make depend on the skill of our role model. For example, if our role model for driving a car had hit everything in sight, we might have made a different assumption about how easy driving was. The problem in comparing driving with project management is that a project gone astray is not as obvious as a car hitting another. So, often we can't assess or evaluate good project management skills. We may see poor project management skills and assume them to be good ones, which leads us in wrong directions and to false expectations. After all, if we never see good project management, we have difficulty in assessing good ones from bad ones. Like riding with a good driver, we immediately assume we know good project management when we see it. Well, so does upper management!

OUR TRADITIONAL APPROACH

We have learned well from poor project management in the past. We have learned so well, in fact, that we have developed a traditional approach with built-in safeguards for ineffective project management skills. So universal is this traditional approach that it can be seen in every organization and with every consulting company. There are distinctive fingerprints that this approach leaves on projects and in organizations. These fingerprints are so predictive of poor project management skills that they can be easily identified. Let's talk about five fingerprints of our traditional approach to project management: contingency time, directionless flight, budget busters, no endings, and taking the easy road.

Contingency Time: "How much time do you think it will take to get it done?" an ineffective project manager is asked. Mentally, a predictable math model begins to emerge. Subconsciously it sounds like this: "Let's see...I can probably get it done in a week, but that's if everything goes well and there are no surprises. But that seldom happens so I'll add contingency time. Let's say the project will take two weeks. That should be enough time; besides, if everything goes easy, I can look like a hero if I deliver it ahead of schedule." So, the ineffective project manager says, "Two weeks...plus or minus a couple of days (adding an extra contingency)."

There appears to be no standardization in the multiplier used for contingency time. This seems to be more consistent among many past experiences in dealing with ineffective project management. In some organizations, the multiplier may be two-times. In others, it may be as high as 4-times. But, in *every* organization with ineffective project management, contingency time is used to pad poor project management skills.

Let's say for our purposes that the contingency time multiplier is just two-times the estimated project time. What does this mean to an organization? It is simple mathematics. If it takes twice as long as it would to use effective project management skills, it costs that organization twice as much in money and resources. If I can do a project with zero waste in one week and that equals $4,000, an ineffectively managed project would take two weeks and cost $8,000. Let's say that an ineffective project manager completes 25 projects that year (50 working weeks divided by two weeks for each project). That equals $200,000 in project costs to that organization. This is compared to $100,000 that effectively managed projects would cost. Then you need to half the number of projects that can be completed in a year to calculate the total waste in this example. How many project managers who add in contingency time does your organization have?

DUFFY

"Let me see...on the last project I was two weeks short...The time before that I was three weeks long..."

"That means that I'm either two-thirds right or three-halves wrong!"

What would be the cost paid out to a consulting business that makes its money off projects? Simple math gets stalled here because of varying billing rates. But calculate it this way: if the project takes twice as long to accomplish due to ineffective project management, the consulting company will get twice as much money. No loss...mathematically for the consulting firm. But put yourself in the shoes of the customer that is buying project management time from the consulting firm. If consulting company A can do my project in one week at one weeks charge rate and company B uses contingency time to correct for ineffective project management and says it will take two weeks at two weeks charge rate, which consultant am I going to hire? It doesn't take a mathematician to calculate which consulting firm will get the job, does it?

Directionless Flight: Have you ever watched an eagle soar in the thermals? Beautiful, isn't it. In a seemingly effortless manner, the eagle glides in the upswell of air. Circling, circling, climbing, then declining, the eagle becomes a picture of tranquillity and efficiency of motion. But in reality, the eagle has nowhere it needs to go. The only responsibilities it has are to eat, sleep, and have little eagles. This is very different from us. In our jobs, we get paid to accomplish something. We do not get paid to glide in the thermals.

What is directionless flight in a project? It occurs when nothing is getting accomplished—when there is no measurable progress to the project's goal. Ineffectively managed projects always hit periods where advancement seems to be stalled or backwards. These periods occur because someone lost focus on what was necessary to accomplish, got misdirected, was diverted by another task, forgot a step, or made everyone else wait for something to happen. These stalled periods might also occur when an unforeseen issue, resource need, or roadblock springs up. These periods of directionless flight are fingerprints of ineffective project management. They waste resources, time, and money. In this case, it's a good thing that ineffective project managers also use contingency time. It allows excessive time to be available for the periods of directionless flight when nothing gets done.

Often, this waste is a product of not starting off with a clear definition of the project or not determining the objectives that need to be accomplished. Starting off without a clear definition is like going on a trip without knowing your final destination. Consequently, you never get there. Like Lewis Carroll's Cheshire Cat says to Alice, "If you don't know where you're going, any road will do." Just as critical is that there is no time demand to get there. But time costs money...real money.

Also, if no project objectives have been established, important milestones, accomplishments, and limitations are missed. Consequently, projects don't achieve what they need to, important dates are missed, and the project comes in over budget. The roots of directionless flight are traditional in ineffective project management.

Budget Busters: There is a common ailment in over 95 percent of the capital plans in American companies—nothing ever gets done on or under budget. That's why requests for budget overruns are so common. I knew one project manager who worked for a Fortune 100 company who was very skilled in project management. The company he worked for, however, was not accustomed to this level of skill. When a major project he was working on reached 70 percent completion, his manager confronted him and asked when he would be seeking an overrun approval. The manager was shocked when informed that everything was fine. Not wanting to lose out on any available capital moneys, though, the project manager was forced into seeking funds he didn't need. In this company, doing something in budget was too violent of a paradigm shift and it disrupted the status quo political power process. Strange!

Why do projects that are ineffectively managed so often run over budget? The major reasons are lack of project definition and poor planning. For one, directionless flight is expensive. Planning says that when you first seek funding for a project, you actually know what the costs will be. This is very rare. Most projects in American businesses get caught in the "no-patience" trap. If the project is such a good idea in the first place, it becomes a race to the bank. Planning in this mindset only uses time, which can be made up at some other place in the process. Unfortunately, without planning, the budget becomes more guesswork. And these guesses are seldom correct. Another confounder is that no one wants to propose a project that raises financial eyebrows. It's called "low balling." Besides, when the true costs become known, returning for cost overrun approvals is a common and accepted practice.

No Endings: This is another traditional fingerprint of ineffective project management. Projects can literally go on forever. The Central Utah Project (CUP) is an excellent example. The original project was conceived in Congress to supply critically needed water to the heaviest populated area of the State of Utah. It began in the 1950s. More than forty years later, the project still is not complete and is costing taxpayers millions each year. "I guess it's okay when it's the government and money never runs out," a business leader once said of the CUP. "But dealing with limited resources and focusing on the bottom line, we have to do projects differently in business." I've got a bit of reality for this business leader—it happens all the time in business just like it happens in government-funded projects.

What else happens when a project never gets done? Another manifestation is that these projects tend to get lost within other, more critical or urgent projects. They just weave into the fabric of other projects.

Taking the Easy Road: Every project has two levels of object-ives—easy ones and hard ones. Ideally, for a project to be completed, all of these objectives must be accomplished. Not so in an ineffectively managed project. Reaching objectives follows a predictable path. The easy tasks get done quickly and are widely and loudly announced to upper management. The hard tasks don't get done and become lost in the effort.

In another example, a major improvement project was planned and begun in a large manufacturing facility. There were three important objectives of the project: to purchase an overhead crane, to take down the old crane, and to install the new one. Purchasing the crane was an easy task. It took three people acting separately. An engineer selected the crane, a buyer purchased it, and an accounting clerk paid for it, once the bill was received. Scheduling the downtime to take down the old crane and install the new one, however, was hard. Accomplishing these tasks required a lot of communication and coordination. Many people needed to be involved including purchasing, contracting, production, production scheduling, marketing, maintenance, safety, and human resources. The new crane was selected in less than a week, purchased the next week, and received two months later. After the bill was received, it was paid within 30 days. Lacking a well-protected place to store the new crane awaiting installation, it was placed on the ground about 200 feet from the building where it would be used. Two years later the crane still sat there. Exposed to the elements, it no longer appeared new. In this case, the hard task never got done.

SPECIALIZED SKILLS

Effective project management is the application of very specific and specialized skills. True, good project management includes concepts that are generally thought of as commonplace management skills. These "boilerplate" skills include planning, communication, attention to detail, coordination, measuring results and plotting progress, and salesmanship. But the specific skills that complement effective project management, although similar to general management skills, are very refined and specific to managing projects. One cannot assume that if one is an effective manager of an organization, a budget, or people, then he or she will have the necessary skills to manage projects. This assumption has landed countless projects on the rocks and the careers of good managers and professionals in limbo. Make no mistake about it; project management skills are highly specific and tailored to meet the needs of project management. To an effective manager who learns project management skills, these skills become a separate drawer of tools that he or she only uses for projects.

Remember our earlier example of the experienced professional of twenty years who joined the consulting company? This is an all too common story based on this assumption trap—project management skills equal general management skills. They are *not* equal. Think of the difference between the two in terms of a military pilot who is making the transition into military retirement as an airline pilot. The skills necessary for flying a supersonic jet fighter do not qualify that pilot to take the helm of a jumbo jet with 350 people on board. Piloting an F-16 and a 747 require very different skills. For an airline to make such a mistake would be disastrous. They recognize this and require extensive training and a form of apprentice training before the pilot sits in the left seat. We passengers recognize and appreciate the difference and the level of extensive training required before any pilot gets to captain *our* flight. This is exactly the case in comparing project management skills to even excellent general management skills. The two are just very different.

But in what ways are the skills of management and project management different? Isn't one just a refinement of another? In some ways, yes. However, in the mechanisms and sequences used, it is very different. Look to the above example for clarity. Piloting a single engine plane, the pilot is the navigator, the crew, and the only pilot. It is, for the most part, a one-person crew. The pilot depends on himself or herself. This is a lot like management. A manager is responsible for what he or she gets done. If an important accomplishment is not achieved, they are chiefly responsible.

Likewise, being a pilot of a jumbo jet and crew is very different. Not only is the pilot responsible for himself or herself, he or she is also responsible for the coordination of the crew, communications with the tower, keeping the customers happy, making sure the plane is perfect for flight, take-offs, and landings. The pilot's holistic responsibilities far outreach his or her piloting responsibilities. So far, in fact, that the management responsibilities far exceed specific piloting responsibilities. This is similar to how it is to manage a project. It isn't about managing oneself; it is about managing a project that involves many limitations, resources, and personnel. Project management skills are more specific than those of general management.

FAILURE POINTS AND PREVENTION

So, where are the common failure points in project management? Truthfully, they are found throughout the entire management system, but they tend to congregate in a few of the major areas. Later we will introduce an effective approach, a model for managing projects. But, first of all, let's take a look at the traditional steps in project management so that we can identify the failure points and focus on the simple means of prevention.

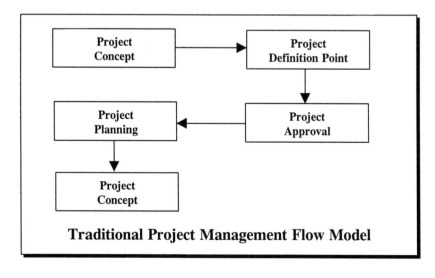

Traditional Project Management Flow Model

Oddly enough, each of these five steps in the traditional project management model can be a major failure point. Let's look at what can happen in each step, why it can happen, and how it can be prevented.

Project Concept: Project concepts have a high probability of being highly idealistic. "Gee, wouldn't it be great if we were able to modify this process so that we can make twice as much material with higher quality, use less raw material and labor, and do it in half the time?" This is no joking matter. Often, this is a common beginning point for a project concept. Here's another one: "If we want to be successful in our bid for this project, we need to do everything everybody else is going to propose but at half the cost." The fallout of an overly idealistic project concept is that everything past this step is a disappointment—caused, of course, by reality.

For this reason, project concepts really need to be a negotiated, team process. One person has his or her perspective, knowledge limitations, and biases. When you add diversity to developing project concepts through a team-oriented approach, a lot of idealism and naiveté is avoided. Project concepts must never be pulled out of the air and chiseled on the wall. Having a formalized process for identifying project concepts for an organization always assures that both the high-road and low-road project concepts that are pulled out of the air for consideration and refinement are subject to reality checks, organizational limitations, and personnel limitations.

Project Definition: This can be a two-way failure point. A definition for a project can be too short, making it not well enough defined. A definition can also be so detailed that it serves as an anvil around the neck of the project manager. Both types of definitions can be terribly destructive to a project.

A project definition that lacks sufficient detail is in danger of taking on a life of its own. An example is the Central Utah Project (CUP) that had an unofficial project definition stating, "to assure sufficient water reserves exist to meet the economic needs of the Wasatch front area." The key words and phrases that lack measurable specificity include "sufficient," "reserves," "meet the economic needs," and "the

Wasatch front area." What is "sufficient" to me will certainly be different to you. If you are a career bureaucrat, chances are your definition will be widely different than ours in the private sector (as supported by a lot of history). Likewise, what is a "reserve?" Is it enough to meet demand or what is always ready in storage? When we look at "meet the economic needs" when do we take a pulse? Is a baseline in 1963 okay or do we have to consider 2025? And lastly, what defines "the Wasatch front area?" Is it the heavily populated area around Salt Lake City or does it also include the farming communities that exist in 100 miles in every direction? Having too little specific, measurable information in the project definition assures that the project will go on like the Eveready® bunny, as long as power or funds (or patience) exist.

What can be wrong with adding too many specifics to a project definition? Ideally, a project definition only states the major deliverable or project purpose. If everything that the project is supposed to do is stated in the project definition, what happens if, like most projects, all the lights-and-whistles don't come about? For example, if a project purpose is to move a working group from one building to the next, why would you add details including how the move is to be accomplished, who is responsible, what advantages the move will provide, etc? These are "fluid" aspects of the project that will be identified, and possibly modified, within the project planning and implementation phases.

How can this failure point concerning project definitions be prevented? Follow the KISS principle, which we will talk about in detail in Chapter 2.

Project Approval: This is a very tricky step. It is also one of the most common failure points in project management. How so? Let's draw some pictures to illustrate some potential problems.

Picture #1 –The "Yes-Kinda-Maybe" Approval: Because a project is considered urgent, approval to go ahead is given with incomplete information, very little planning, and very soft information about the needed budget. When details begin to be known and communicated, the approving management begins a continual effort to micro-manage every discovery and detail of the project, often renegotiating issues over and over again. These types of projects are always uphill battles and commonly never get completed.

Picture #2 –The "Hide and Seek" Approval: A project is considered important to a project leader. Knowing that the needed budget will be significantly larger than what is available, he "customizes" the budget to please management and get quick approval. The project manager knows that there is no way it can be done within the approved budget. Then a date is set to make the first request for overruns. These types of projects are frustrating to all involved, including the project team and upper management.

Picture #3 –The "Shell Game" Approval: Let's say a project will cost over $1 million ($1M). The budget approval authority of the particular level in the organization that wants the budget to go ahead is $1M. To gain approval, the project is broken into two projects that are each less than $1M. To make the deception not so obvious, often two different project managers are assigned to each sub-project. Now an important project depends on the effective working relationship and communication between two distinct project managers. These types of projects tend to become stalemated by lack of communication and coordination. They are seldom accomplished in-step and without great organizational discomfort.

DUFFY

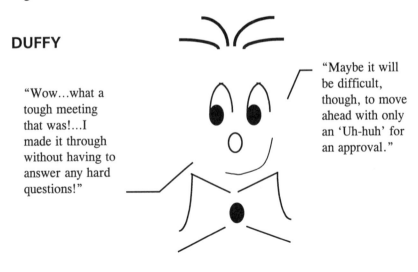

"Wow...what a tough meeting that was!...I made it through without having to answer any hard questions!"

"Maybe it will be difficult, though, to move ahead with only an 'Uh-huh' for an approval."

Picture #4 –The "Never Say Yes" Approval: A project is sub-mitted for approval, but upper management has great difficulty just saying, "Yes." Instead, they give the ultimate authority to the project manager, and then get out of the way. This is usually a form of management trepidation. So, the project continues with tentative approvals, or partial approvals, as it continues. The management of the project becomes a constant effort of seeking and acquiring approvals. This is very inefficient and usually results in the beginning project manager not being able to finish the project. By choice or directive, project managers of these types of projects tend to be replaced a lot.

Project Approval Failures

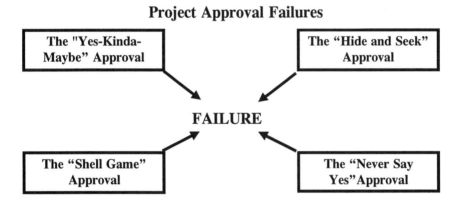

Project approvals can be swift, empowering actions. Commonly, however, they more closely resemble a slow painful death, or at least a near-fatal disease of management uncertainty. How can this be avoided? It is too simple to just say—decisive and empowered upper management. Looking at the state of management in America today, this may very well be an oxymoron. In many instances, though, the approval one gets has a high correlation to how well the project is defined, planned, and known by the project manager. In other words, clear plans have a high chance of getting clear approvals.

Project Planning: This is often the biggest failure point in project management. Factually, we don't tend to plan very well. This isn't a statement only about projects or work, this is a statement about life. Whether we are planning the Cub Scout Fund Raiser, working with the neighborhood crime watch program, planting a garden, building a boat in the basement, planning our investment portfolio or retirement income, in most cases we don't plan worth a damn.

There is a ratio that some economists use. It is a ratio of individual economic status in America and it is simply called the 3-10-60-27 ratio. Economists know that 3 percent of the population are *very* well off financially, 10 percent are well off, and 60 percent live within their means. This latter group is often defined as living within 10 percent of its income. The remaining 27 percent represent those in our population who require some kind of financial public assistance to get by.

There are two critically important points the economists tell us about this ratio. First, it has been constant for more than 100 years. Second, if all the money were somehow leveled out among all members of the population, some economists argue that this same ratio would reappear in seven and one half years. Obviously, then, the ratio exists due to some dynamic that exists in our society. What is that dynamic? I would argue that the dynamic is planning.

I think you can use these same ratios to make some generalizations about planning. Let's say that 3 percent make planning an art form. They plan everything, document the plan, track completion via measurement and re-plan at regular intervals. The next 10 percent also plan well, but their devotion to planning and the height of their goals are not as great as the 3 percent. They also are willing to risk less. Let's say that 60 percent of the population plan minimally. They also risk minimally. They plan enough to get by in most cases, but their planning often falls short or misses the mark entirely. That would leave us with the 27 percent who don't plan well at all and seldom have the assets to take any risks.

Now, if we examine this ratio, we see that good planning is an important skill that is not broadly utilized in our population. We have to wonder how important is good planning in successful project management? Factually, it isn't just important—it is critical. Yet it is such a common practice to start projects with the cavalier belief that, once started, a project will bring itself to completion. But without planning, it seldom does. Without planning, a project never reflects back on efficient management, utilization of resources, or minimal cycle times.

Planning, therefore, is a critical skill for project managers. Chapter 3 has been dedicated to the subject of project planning. But if planning and organization is a recognized weakness in your skills, you might consider subsidizing your learning even further with some additional information on building planning skills.

Project Implementation: Failure points in project implementation have specific roots. These failure points include not anticipating problems, not being observant of problems or changes, not reacting to changes, premature implementation (also called "flying by the seat of your pants"), communication failures, surprising sponsors, not learning from history, or deserting the plan.

THE EIGHT ROOTS OF PROJECT IMPLEMENTATION FAILURE

Root 1–Not anticipating problems: Reality says that no matter how good the plan, problems will still spring up. But telling oneself that problems will not happen because the plan was done well is an easy trap to fall into. Therefore, projects are often implemented with a glazed over attitude. This is a fool's paradise. Without anticipating problems, reaction time will also be considerably slower. Effective project managers can never fall into this fairy tale world that threatens the rapid dispersal of problems. Efficient project implementation is all about rapid response and resolution of problems to unexpected events.

Root 2–Not being observant of problems or changes: Some problems and changes are so obvious that they cannot be ignored. Others seem small but grow in magnitude if they are not addressed in a timely fashion. Generally, the better the planning effort is, the less likely a large-magnitude problem or change should occur. In other words, the better the plan, the more subtle problems or changes will be. But even subtle problems and changes in the project have a nasty habit of growing exponentially if they are left undetected or not dealt with. This is where constant vigilance is required for effective project management.

Root 3–Not reacting to changes: Some changes that occur in project implementation are no big deal and can be ignored. But these are extremely rare. In more than 99 percent of encountered changes, some response or reaction is necessary. It may be as simple as acknowledging the change happened and communicating that no impact due to it is anticipated to the project team. It may require extensive reaction and plan modification. The important point is that when changes occur, some reaction is almost always required from an effective project manager.

Root 4–Premature implementation: Have you ever started an activity before you were actually ready? Of course—we all have. It's a risky situation to place ourselves in. It is far more obvious that we made a mistake by starting something prematurely after we have started it than before. If it were obvious before, we simply wouldn't ever get caught in this trap. An effective project manager knows this and realizes that it is best to implement a project only if adequate work and attention to detail are accomplished in the previous steps of project management.

Root 5–Communication failures: The lifeblood of effective project implementation is communication. Whenever communication fails, implementation falters—it is a simple and direct relationship. The key person in communication is always the project manager. It is a prime responsibility that falls directly on his or her shoulders, no one else's. So, of course, if communication causes implementation problems, the cause of this failure of communication is obvious and undeniable.

Root 6–Surprising sponsors: Normally, sponsors are those individuals who authorize a project and provide the necessary resources so that it can be accomplished. There is a simple rule here: *never, never, NEVER* surprise a sponsor. Surprising a sponsor can result in the withdrawal of support or resources. These are deathblows to a project. Prevention can be simple—communicate effectively with your sponsors. I say "can be simple" because some news is not exactly easy to deliver. Maybe you screwed up. Maybe the news is just bad, like you're going to need more budget. No matter what, if the project is worth doing, bad news must be communicated as well as good. And guess whose responsibility it is to communicate with the sponsors?

Root 7–Not learning from history: History has a strange habit of repeating itself, but *only* if one makes the same mistakes. Having a problem appear once can be disastrous enough. Having the same problem occur again because the information was not captured and learned is ineffective and ultimately wasteful. The saying, "Fool me once, shame on you—but fool me twice, shame on me" speaks of this need to learn from history. Project management is no different in this respect than life. We are learning creatures. We must learn what experience teaches us, and by our learning, avoid problems the next time.

Root 8–Deserting the plan: No matter how bad things are, things can only get worse in project implementation if you pitch out all the work that has gotten you to this point. In implementation, the plan becomes the most important aspect of the project. It may be flawed, it may have problems, or it may be incomplete, but it is the roadmap that offers the only known path to success. Throwing out the plan due to frustration, ignorance, or some other reason will almost assuredly spell doom for the project. This is another reason to plan well.

Roots of Implementation Failure

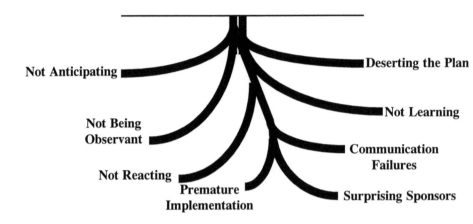

Not Anticipating

Not Being Observant

Not Reacting

Premature Implementation

Deserting the Plan

Not Learning

Communication Failures

Surprising Sponsors

DIFFERENCES IN VISION AND PERCEPTIONS

There is a point that needs to be stressed in discussing project management skills. Management's perception of project management is very different from that of an effective project manager. One is a view from outside, the other from inside. Management sees the results (or lack of results) and the statistical measures of the project. The project manager sees all the details, the to-do list, the problem-solving efforts, and the communication. From the top, management sees the holistic project. From inside, the project manager sees all the pieces that comprise the project. Management judges the success and progress of the project largely by perception. The project manager manages the success of the project by fact, schedule, and commitment. Management visualizes the completed project. From inside, the project manager looks at how all the parts fit together into a successful project. Management focuses on completion. The project manager knows that, upon completion, he or she will move onto the next project. They focus on the present. Management focuses on milestones that are successfully made. The project manager focuses on reaching those milestones. Management sees what part of the budget has been spent. The project manager looks at what part of the budget is left. Management and project managers have very different perspectives on the life of a project.

Why is it important to point out these differences? Too often, buried in the project management detail from the inside, one forgets that these differences exist. It is too convenient to begin assuming that management sees what the project manager sees. This can cause two dangerous problems—myopic paranoia and surprised sponsors. Myopic paranoia occurs when the project manager becomes convinced that management sees everything he or she is doing or not doing. In such a situation it is natural to begin to look over your shoulder a lot, wait for reactions or advice from management, or begin to provide unnecessary details and confessions to management that invite increased micromanagement and loss of management faith. It's a form of self-destruction or project unraveling.

We've already introduced the subject of surprising project or resource sponsors. This occurs when a project manager seeks actively to avoid ongoing contact with the sponsors throughout the project. But, forgetting or avoiding that contact with sponsoring management limits the project manager's perspective of project management. After all, the feeling is that if the sponsors see and know everything the project manager does, why is it necessary to communicate what is already known? In such a state of withheld information, critical information is missed along the route to project completion and sponsors become confused. Confusion is a precursor to surprise. No matter what is communicated, discovered, or perceived in confusion, it's surprising. Remember the rule: *Never surprise a sponsor!*

A young environmental engineer working for a Fortune 75 company was given a very important project—to design and install a significant upgrade of a pollution control system. The best available control technology had been discarded as too expensive to build and run, but the facility's management had remained committed to environmental leadership. In the meantime, a new control theory had surfaced. Management believed that if this worked, it could revolutionize the control technologies for this air pollutant. The laboratory tests up to that point were all positive. The bench-top, scale-up experiments had worked flawlessly. So it was decided to forgo the expensive pilot plant stage-up. The bench-top experiments would be used to best calculate the design. Flexibility would be designed into the project so that final refinement and optimization could be done when the system was being taken through its start-up. Sure, skipping the traditional pilot plant step would add some risk, but the cost savings and time savings were significant and worth the small costs for installing flexibility in the design.

An impressive in-house team was assembled under the young environmental engineer's leadership. The ambitious timetable would take the project from concept to start-up in only 16 months. Four million dollars million was earmarked for the project.

Although young, the environmental engineer who was named project manager had good communication and interpersonal skills. The project team and the mentoring of the engineering manager would reinforce his organizational and planning skills. But the young project manager knew that this was a critical project to the company and a lot of money was at risk and it would be relatively easy to blow a project of this size.

A couple of years earlier, the company had had the foresight to standardize the project management process and tools used at the facility. They had invested heavily in software and training for both engineering and management alike. Since that time, the project management and management leadership skills of all managers had been greatly enhanced. Their project management history had improved from one that was always over budget, behind schedule, and overly micromanaged to one that was regularly meeting budget constraints and making deadlines. This new project would indeed be a test of the company's commitment and progress.

The project was carefully defined and clear, measurable goals and objectives were agreed upon. The budget needs were carefully broken down and allocated to specific project deliverables. Extensive team planning resulted in task breakdowns, assigned responsibilities, and finally, a timeline in graphical form. Everything was made visible for the project team and management. Regular project team meetings discussed and resolved every detail and expectation. Management received regular briefings on progress, problems, changes, and costs. Employees were kept up-to-date via a special newsletter that was developed and published. Members of the project team spent significant time traveling and on the telephone assuring and communicating design and delivery needs. All departments—including design engineering, process engineering, operations, maintenance, safety and environmental, purchasing, accounting and accounts payable, computer systems, and instrumentation—worked together in a well-orchestrated effort.

Process hazard analyses were performed on all aspects of the project. Work procedures were begun, revised, refined, and finalized. Safeguards were designed, critiqued, redesigned, refined, and adopted. Worker training was begun and remained continual throughout the worker's involvement in every aspect of the project. Engineering walk-throughs were conducted. Pre-start-up safety reviews were completed. The process shakedown began. Everything worked as designed. Fifteen months and twenty-two days after the project kickoff sent a newly formed project team scampering confidently into a major investment, the pollution control device came up and worked.

Was this a surprise? Many who have had similar experiences or seen projects of this magnitude struggle and fail would say "Yes." A young, minimally experienced environmental engineer just couldn't accomplish such a team-oriented feat, on time and in such a tight budget. It just couldn't be done. Well, I'm here to tell you that it was done and that it was no surprise to this company or its management. No surprise at all!

Obviously, this example says a lot about project management skills and how those skills become part of an organization's culture. Herein lies the key to this example.

OBJECTIVES

Successful project management is not brain surgery. It is not a skill that takes twelve years to learn and master. It doesn't require extensive or elaborate software programs to be done well. Effective project management is as simple as using a management process and understanding why following the process is important. The *how* of project management is a project management process that works. But you can't forget the *why* element. Not knowing why makes the process rely on faith. And face it, we are terribly curious—which is a nice way to say we seldom have faith.

The objectives of this book are to provide that process for managing projects and to make sure you understand why it works. This process is a weaving together of many project management tools, flowcharts, step-sequences, and individual processes that have been described and refined over the last forty years. If you look into project management texts and articles, of which there are many, you will literally be overrun by what each author claims is the best method. I don't do that.

Long ago, I realized that one method is seldom head-and-shoulders better than others. And with the boom in project management software, the "I'm Best" claims are just beginning to move toward another crescendo.

Long ago, I learned something else that is useful. When you are at a banquet table, never take just one! That's why I've picked from many methods to arrive at this process for successful project management.

But, as I stated earlier, you also need to know *why*. Most project management texts stop there. After all, they're the experts—they must know why. You should just follow their advice and method, right? But I don't see things that way. If you are to have faith that any process will work and be convinced that it has value in your application, you simply have to know the *why* element. I've brought up a lot about the *whys* already. I will continue to explore that element more throughout this book.

2

AN OVERVIEW OF PROJECT MANAGEMENT

I have a friend who happens to be "checkbook challenged—he has great difficulty in managing his checkbook. This isn't a new discovery. His wife recognized this trait more than twenty years ago, immediately after they were married when he made an innocent declaration, "It's okay if it doesn't balance...just round it off and call it okay. Plus a little this month...minus a little next, it all balances out."

"What?" was her shocked response. You see, she is *not* "checkbook challenged." In fact, she is "detail gifted." Needless to say, they have an agreement that has lasted them (and their marriage) for many years. She manages the checkbook and he keeps his hands off of it. Good deal!

This same friend just happens to be a great project manager. What? How can someone be incapable of managing a simple checkbook and be extremely effective and efficient at managing detailed, complex projects? That's a good question. A good place to start looking for the answer is with project management itself.

WHAT IS A PROJECT?

"My life's a project," I once heard a professional colleague of mine say. Well, not exactly. If it were, nothing would ever be in steady state. But, this is an important place for us to begin. What is a project? How is project management different from how we manage everyday activities? In a holistic sense, a project is any activity that is not routinely performed. It's something that goes through a dedicated, concentrated rework or revision. Starting a business would definitely be considered a project. Defining and coordinating a major change in the way chemicals enter the workplace would also be a project. Designing and putting on a fundraiser for the PTA at your child's school would also be a project. Filling the gas tank of your car, driving to work, helping your kids with their homework, performing an industrial hygiene sampling, or completing an accident investigation report are activities that wouldn't be considered projects. In a general sense, a project is anything that is not part of your routine activities.

DUFFY

"My ex-wife gave me a project once......"

"She told me to get lost!"

From a work perspective, the definition of a project becomes much easier to get our hands on. A project is 1) nonroutine, 2) has a formal purpose or goal, 3) has a beginning and ending (or intended ending) date, and 4) generally has a budget restraint.

Project Definition

- **Nonroutine**
- **Has a Purpose or Goal**
- **Has a Beginning and Ending**
- **Has a Budget Rest**

Using this simple definition, projects include such activities as environmental remediation efforts, contracted jobs, new process or equipment installations, writing or coordinating environmental permit applications, major revisions of facility safety manuals, rewriting employee handbooks, implementing contractor safety programs, making major changes in management philosophy, writing books or articles for publication, research projects, accomplishing major training efforts, etc. When you stop and look at what we do from this perspective, a great number of our day-to-day activities are taken up by accomplishing projects.

From a simplified perspective—and for the sake of definition—when a project is done, it's done. From start to finish, that effort is unique. Nonprojects, on the other hand, will be done over and over again as part of routine tasks.

ASPECTS OF A PROJECT

From a management perspective, there are four manageable aspects of every project—the project itself, the allocated budget, the assigned time, and the project value. The project itself as a manageable entity is obvious. Something needs to be accomplished. Getting from nothing to something requires a managed effort. This aspect includes project definition and planning, acquiring the necessary approvals, acquiring and coordinating resources, communicating, scheduling, and a number of management activities.

The second aspect of a project is keeping costs within the allocated budget. This includes more than money management. It extends from identifying the realistic and near-accurate costs prior to the project initition (which is a skill unto itself), acquiring the necessary budget as identified, and managing the budget throughout the project. None of these are easy management skills.

The third aspect of a project is managing time. Like the budget management process, time management begins with identifying a realistic and attainable time structure for the project. This time structure must meet management or business expectations and must recognize resource coordination and time scheduling. Once determined and approved, the management aspect then addresses scheduling, coordinating, and making time commitments throughout the project.

The last aspect of a project is the one that is most often misunderstood. Projects are *not* simply about accomplishing something. Anyone can place pegs into holes until done. Pegs alone do not justify the project, the budget, the allocation of resources or the time. A project must provide value to that organization. How is this organization going to be better with this project than without? Is accomplishing this project really going to make a difference? Is the project really worth the amount of money, resources, and time committed to it? These are value questions to ask during the project's planning, initiation, and review stages.

A project must provide organizational value. If it's a "Who cares?" issue of questionable worth, it represents a resource waste to that organization, and someone must have the courage to cut it free and do without it. That person may be the project manager. This is a hard concept for us when we look at project management as a means to an end. "Give me a project and I'll get it done." Value means it must make a difference, or provide a definite advantage to the organization. A project must be an integral component of the organization's improvement program. It must provide value.

TEAM CONCEPTS OF PROJECT MANAGEMENT

The project manager is usually a singular commodity; that is, usually there is only one manager named to each project. This makes the issue of responsibility and accountability for the project much easier for management. It also serves as a designated focal point for any questions, communication, and problems that concern that project.

But the real power that drives a project is the input, coordination, participation, and results provided by everyone who plays a part in the project. Successful projects are team-oriented. The term "team" implies that everyone works together for the success of the project. Team members are not pawns to be moved around the board at the direction and will of the project manager. Team members need to be willing contributors.

Where are teams used in a project? Planning teams capture the ideas and input from various functions and specialties. Presentation teams package the project proposal into a form for getting approvals. Design teams work on the technical elements of the project, including the layout, drawings, and computer programming. Development teams establish operating procedures and training for the project, once implemented. Safety and environmental teams, customer liaison or communications teams, project teams, and several other adjunct teams are also used when needed. Certainly, there is an implementation team that gets the job done. Throughout the life of a project, teams spring up, serve a specific purpose, and then dissolve once that aspect of the project is successfully completed.

The project manager must have team leadership skills and all team members need to be skilled in team dynamics. Neither of these skills are givens in today's society. Often they require specialized training in areas such as negotiating, planning, forming and chartering teams, team communications, team dynamics, and conflict resolution.

Let's take a lesson from sports. Not all sports "teams" are really teams. Some have multiple and specialized players, but when play begins, it becomes "every man or woman for themselves." No one shares. No one helps out. No one backs-up or covers another player. We know these "teams" well. They very seldom have long-term success.

On the other hand, there are teams that are really teams. We can recognize it immediately when watching them. Their effort becomes an orchestrated effort. Everyone knows his or her responsibility and the teamwork enhances individual efforts and abilities. The whole effort seems to step up a notch when individuals become a team. They are more successful, they win more often, and they are more fun to watch because they get more fun out of team involvement. This team dynamic is what is needed for a successful project to be completed by a team.

ESTIMATING PROJECT DURATION

From the very beginning, there are two questions that hit: "How long will it take?" and "How much will it cost?" Disinterested people don't ask these questions—it is usually upper management. These questions surface immediately, usually before the project manager or team has thought out the answers.

Is that fair? Sure it is. Upper management is responsible for running the organization and it needs information about ongoing projects to do that. On the other hand, upper management also knows that a project manager couldn't possibly know the answer to those two questions this early in the project life. So what are they really asking? What management is really asking is fundamental: "Can we afford this project?" and "When can we put the project completion on our calendar?" We must realize that management is not necessarily seeking finite answers. Sure, they want better than rough estimates—they want close, but not exact, numbers. Because of that, estimating accurately is an important skill for a project manager to be able to do quickly and well.

Cost estimates come from experience. What does it cost to put up a 50-foot by 80-foot building? What does a typical local exhaust ventilation system cost? What does one month of design engineering time cost? These are merely mental calculations made from experience.

Estimating the time a project will take is more of a challenge. How is it done? The good news is that you are not the first project manager to be faced with this challenge. In fact, project time estimation has become quite a science. It has been honed into a simple formula that a project manager can use.

Estimated

Project = <u>**Optimum Time + 4 x Most Likely + Most Pessimistic**</u>

Time   6

The formula is simple. Determine a range of time the project could reasonably take to accomplish. Let's say it could take between 6 and 10 months. Be honest with yourself. If you were betting (to a great extent, you are), what is the most likely amount of time the project will take? Let's say from your past experience of doing projects like this, and from knowing the comfort level in this organization, that the most likely time is a little more than 7 months. Plug everything into this simple formula and you get:

Example

Project = <u>**6 Months + (4 x 7.25 Months) + 10 Months**</u>
                                  6

Project = <u>**6 + 29 + 10**</u> = **7.5 Months**
                  6

Estimating with fair accuracy is really not rocket science. But accuracy is relative and very vulnerable to our misinterpretation of what management is asking. They don't want to know the exact numbers and dates. That is unrealistic and they know that. But, they do want a project manager to have the skills to answer the more fundamental questions with a certain level of accuracy. In most situations, plus or minus 15 percent is acceptable. Plus or minus 50 percent, on the other hand, is not.

APPROVALS

There are some facts about approvals that project managers need to understand and accept: 1) approvals come in degrees and steps; 2) there is no such thing as a one-time, stand-alone, get-out-of-my-way, no-strings-attached approval; 3) when you get an approval, there are responsibilities that go along with it; and 4) an "Okay, go ahead," really isn't full approval at all.

Approvals Come in Degrees and Steps: Depending on the project type, company history, and expectations of upper management in an organization, approvals may be few and simple or multiple and continuous. In other words, an approval can be as simple as a head-nod or it can be like going back to the bank for a home construction loan at $100 intervals. The latter is an extreme analogy, but where there is great anxiety or fear on the part of upper management with projects, the approval process can seem tedious.

At a minimum, there are two levels or steps in the approval process—the preliminary and the final approval. The preliminary approval gives the project manager the go-ahead to further develop the project and determine specific needs and schedules. This preliminary approval happens pretty early in the project life, just after concept and definition. The final approval is given when management has reached a comfort level with the project requirements and risks. The final approval is necessary before a project manager gets seriously involved in the nuts-and-bolts of project implementation.

There Is No Such Thing as a One-Time, Stand-Alone, We'll-Get-Out-of-Your-Way, No-Strings-Attached Approval: Every project manager I've met wishes that he or she could receive unconditional approval. The fact is that there is no such thing. Approvals are never one-time. As we stated earlier, you have to expect to return for other approvals as the project proceeds. No approvals are stand-alone. There are many interfaces with upper management throughout the project life. Sponsoring management never entirely gets out of a project manager's way, even after a project is approved. And, of course, there are always strings attached to the approval. Most approvals resemble a spider web of attachments, requirements, and encumberances.

When You Get an Approval, There Are Responsibilities That Go Along With It: By approving a project, sponsoring management places certain responsibilities on the project manager that are specific and expected. These responsibilities include following the organization's established protocols and procedures in the accomplishment of the project. They also include returning for any additional approvals and, certainly, keeping the sponsoring management up to speed on the project—it's problems and changes. A project manager is an organizational team player who builds trust and commitment and must work well within the organization. He or she cannot assume the role of a military general who seeks to divide and conquer in accomplishing the approved project goal. Obviously, fiscal responsibilities come with approvals as do responsibilities for keeping the project on track time-wise. It is also common to add other responsibilities the sponsoring management feels appropriate within the approval process, such as completing pervious projects first, closing out accounts, and establishing regulatory communication.

An "Okay, Go Ahead," Really Isn't Full Approval At All: Any project manager who thinks that receiving a rousing approval to his or her project means "go ahead" is naïve. In reality, an approval means, "Move forward and keep going as long as I feel comfortable within the limitations and additional approvals I have designated." Actually, the word "approval" has a complex meaning in terms of project management. It is never simple or straightforward and its nuances must be well understood by an effective project manager.

The way a project manager seeks approvals is unique to an organization's culture. An organization's culture is a collection of the unwritten rules that govern it. Because of the uniqueness of an organization's culture, the approval process can be very tricky and very seldom is it written down. The process may include the requirement of a formal presentation, including using audiovisual materials and handouts. In the more formal organizations, these presentations are addressed by the culture, as in who is invited and who isn't. Other, less formal organizational cultures have much less stringent formal project approval means. Some approvals can be as informal as "come and talk to me" or a nod of the head in the hallway.

But even in the most informal environments, seeking approval for a project is not as simple as asking. The approval process can be as complex as the project itself. An effective project manager knows what he or she is seeking to accomplish and how to package that information. A project manager must provide the right amount of information for the project. This means "not too much and not too little." Sponsoring management's time is valuable, don't waste it by not having the proper information on hand. Providing too much information may be just as harmful as too little because it may invite unanswerable questions or establish a string of micromanagement that will bog down the project later.

What does the project manager want to get from this presentation for project approval? The project manager wants to minimize anxiety; obtain the necessary budget, time, and resources needed; establish a reputation for efficiency and trust; convey reasonable risks without generating undue anxiety or micromanagement; and sell the project's value. Additionally, the project manager needs to establish check-in times for project progression and get those approved; set up communication intervals and formats; and learn of any limitations that will be imposed by sponsoring management, by company history, or by the expectations of organization management. Of course, the project manager also needs to get the go-ahead.

Summary of Approval Goals

- Give enough but not too much information
- Minimize anxiety
- Obtain the necessary budget
- Obtain time and resources needed
- Establish a reputation of efficiency and trust
- Convey reasonable uncertainties and risks
- Sell the project's value
- Establish check-in times
- Determine communication intervals and for mats
- Learn of any limitations
- Get the go-ahead

THE IMPORTANCE OF PLANNING AND SCHEDULING

A new cutting shear was needed in the maintenance shop. The old shear was purchased as surplus, required constant maintenance attention, and just wouldn't do the bigger jobs. It was decided to replace the shear with a state-of-the-art one that had twice the cutting power, was wider, and could do specialized jobs. A project engineer was assigned to the project of purchasing the new shear and getting it up and running. His time was filled with other responsibilities, but he tried to fit this new project into his schedule. He checked on budget, looked for the best shear available, and put the shear out for quote through the Purchasing Department. The quotes were received but sat on his desk waiting for his available time.

A couple of months later, the busy engineer started to review the quotes, but almost all of them had expired and he had to get quotes for them again. Meanwhile, the old shear continued to break down and require a lot of maintenance. Everyone in the maintenance shop had given up and felt that the new shear would *never* come.

The new quotes came and this time the engineer gave them more immediate attention. A shear that met the specifications and was lowest in cost was purchased. The expected delivery time was eight weeks. It took eleven and a half weeks instead. No one from the purchasing company was watching the delivery time, so no one called the supplier to complain. When the shear finally arrived, it was unloaded from the deliver truck but had nowhere to go. The old shear was still in use, and there wasn't enough storage space for the large new shear inside the facility. The new shear ended up being placed on an asphalt area about 100 feet from the building where it would later be installed.

After the second snow storm, one mechanic thought that maybe the new $100,000 piece of equipment should be covered. He and a buddy got a tarp out of the tool crib and covered it. They used duct tape to secure the tarp as well as they could. It seemed a shame to spend that amount of money on a piece of equipment only to have it ruined by the weather.

Spring came, and the tarp covering the unused shear had to be replaced. Other maintenance employees used a large forklift to put the shear up on blocks so it wouldn't be sitting in the water. It had already started to rust in several places. Five months after it was delivered, the new shear was finally moved to replace the old one. It didn't fit in the place where it needed to be. Much equipment had to be moved in order to make room for the new machinery. A safety inspection uncovered several significant safety concerns that needed to be addressed before the new shear could be used, and safe operating procedures had to be written and training, of course, had to be done.

Work requiring the new shear started to back up. During that time, critical work had to be contracted out to another area machine shop that operated a large shear. Finally, the procedures were written, training was accomplished, and the safety concerns were addressed. But due to the weather damage that had occurred since the shear was delivered, it now required service. The service took another two weeks. The rust spots had to be taken to bare metal and repainted. Finally, the shear was ready for use—thirteen months after the project was given to the engineer. No one really wanted to know what poor planning had cost the company—the re-bid, the wasted time at purchasing, the contracted-out work, the service to the equipment, and the costs. In reality, these costs added up to more than half of the initial purchase price of the shear.

"We were just too busy...We lost track of the project because we were swamped." That was the official response. But anyone who knows efficient project management knows the real answer. The shear project fiasco was the result of a lack of planning and scheduling. If the assigned engineer had only taken the time to plan and schedule the project better, it could have been completed in a third of the time and could have saved a lot of money for the company and exasperation for the maintenance department.

I wish that a lack of planning and scheduling were uncommon in project management. But the vast majority of projects—perhaps 90 percent—go through without formal planning and schedule determination. We simply assume that the job will get done with less than dedicated attention. But, over-and-over again we learn that it won't. Think of it this way: If a project is an organizational event that is important enough to require a special budget, special focus of management, special approvals, updates, special actions, focused activities, and high visibility, shouldn't it be important enough to warrant developing a plan and schedule for assuring that it gets done? Seems rather obvious, doesn't it? Unfortunately, in the vast majority of projects, it isn't obvious to those who are assigned leadership.

Look at planning and scheduling like taking a trip from Los Angeles to Boston. The goal is known and the chosen means of transportation, in this case, is personal automobile. So you start out. Without a plan, you have the choice of taking five interstates, four divided highways, a half-dozen two-lane highways, and almost countless rural roads out of Los Angeles. A statistician would say you had a one-in-a-hundred probability of choosing correctly, or a 0.01 chance. Let's say you get lucky and intuitively head out of LA on Interstate 15. Just a hundred miles out of LA, around Barstow, you are faced with five branches in the road. Choosing the right road here is a multiplier to the first probability, or a 1 in 5 or 0.2 times 0.01 chance. If you calculate the probability of making Boston with at least two hundred points of choice along the correct path, the odds of actually making it there would be practically insurmountable. Time or schedule concerns would become secondary to not accomplishing the project goal. This may be an extreme example but it is very appropriate in emphasizing the importance of planning and scheduling to successful project management.

RESOURCES AND COMMITMENT

Few are fortunate enough to be assigned projects that can be done entirely by themselves. Projects are usually much more complex than that, requiring many different and specialized human resources to accomplish. These resources can include drafting or design specialists, legal specialists, purchasing agents, engineers, maintenance workers, contractors, accountants, computer specialists, instrument specialists, ventilation experts, pollution control specialists, and suppliers. Successful project management requires identification, coordination, and scheduling of these various resources. It involves communicating with, seeking input from, and finding solutions with them. Resource management, therefore, is a critical skill that a successful project manager must have. But it isn't a stand-alone skill—it is part of the planning process, the scheduling endeavor, and the communication and problem solving parts of project management. In effect, effective resource management involves all parts of project management.

Managing human resources can be complex. It's like building a team comprised of consummate superstars. Each resource represents a specialty that is needed to make the team successful. Each resource is independently focused—that means he or she knows a specialty and is focused on doing it. Because of this independent focus, managing resources is very challenging. How do you get a great individual player to work in a highly productive team environment? It can be challenging. This is confounded by the fact that projects have a finite duration. In that way, it is unlike bringing together eleven players for a basketball team where, night-after-night and week-after-week, they will practice and play together to perfect the team dynamic. Project resources may play the entire season and never meet or interact with the other resource players. All this falls on the back of the project manager. Coordination and team making out of these varied resources is his or her responsibility.

This is where commitment comes in. Project management isn't for the meek or for those just wanting a part-time activity to fill some dead hours each day. Project management requires a great deal of commitment. But, even more than that, the project manager needs to make that commitment contagious for the entire project team. Successful projects display almost endemic commitment. Originating with the project manager, each resource, each project team member is committed to the success and schedule of that project.

Commitment is not to be confused with support. If everyone is supportive of what has to be done, isn't that enough? How is being supportive different from being committed to a goal? Being supportive means cheering on someone else's efforts. Being commited means being an active participant in the process. There is a joke that emphasizes this point very well. Eating bacon and eggs is an example of the difference between commitment and support. The hen that lays the eggs for your breakfast is supportive of your appetite for bacon and eggs. The pig, however, is committed to it.

COMMUNICATION IN PROJECT MANAGEMENT

Communication is an easy word to use but it is not an easy task to accomplish. Communicating is one of the most difficult things we humans do. Walk down any crowded street. How many people are communicating with each other? Ride in any crowded elevator. Doesn't everyone focus on the movement of lighted floor numbers? People can sit next to each other for an entire athletic event and never speak. Divorce statistics tell us that the number one cause of couples splitting up is a lack of communication. What is the purpose of marriage counseling, encounter groups, support groups, and alcoholics anonymous? Isn't it to find some sort of resolution or healing by getting participants to communicate? But our upbringing and society in general have set up roadblocks to communication. "Don't talk to strangers." "Don't speak until spoken to." "Don't interrupt your father." Communication isn't a simple subject. It can seem confusing, but it is essential to society.

But communication is also a skill that can be learned. We're not talking about public speaking, so get your heart out of your throat. Effective communication isn't really that complex. It's the direct interface with other people and the emotional baggage that makes it so

DUFFY

"He said that the Wednesday after next wasn't good but that in a "couple" past that, I could count on him..."

"So, I scheduled the job for the Friday following that Wednesday. Too bad what he really meant was a couple of *weeks* after that

complex. Factually, communication is no more than letting the right people know what they need to know when they need to know it. More importantly, it is listening to what messages are sent back. Communication is a two-way street. I communicate and you listen; you communicate and I listen. Knowing this, it really isn't that difficult to communicate effectively. It just requires that I know, as a project manager what you need to know to be a successful member of the project team (planning), when you need to know it (schedule), and when to keep my ears open for your input. This is communication. And in project management, it is a vital skill of the project manager.

There is a facet of communication in project management that must be accentuated—that is, the facilitation of effective communication between the project manager and all others involved in the project. There are three points in this facilitation that must be remembered and practiced throughout the project management process. 1) Give and gather information. Not only does the project manager share important information; he or she is the focal point for gathering and sharing information. 2) Gain and test understanding or make agreements. Many communication skills can be used including repeating what you thought you heard, rephrasing the question, or using an analogy or example to clarify your idea. When understandings are not the same as expected or needed, this is the time to gently push for agreement or negotiate a middle-of-the-road position. 3) Determine the necessary actions to take. Communication has a single purpose: it directs or reinforces actions. Put the words and information into action, make changes to plans, follow up on points, share information gained or agreements made, etc., with all people involved in the project.

Facilitating Communication

- Gain and test understanding or make agreements
- Give and gather information
- Determine the necessary actions to take

Communication in project management is crucial. It is necessary for developing the project plan; it sells the project to upper management; it gets the necessary budget and time; it spreads knowledge; it solves problems. It coordinates resources; it keeps others up to date; it moves the project toward completion. Communication must be good, accurate, timely, and two-way for a project to be successful.

TECHNICAL VERSUS PEOPLE SKILLS

When we are hired as engineers, environmental professionals, industrial hygienists, or safety professionals, we are hired for our specialty—our technical knowledge or skills. When a technical person is promoted to a management, lead, or supervisory position, he or she really needs to have some people skills. Here lies a rub in our traditional organizations. Very often when promoted, the technical professional doesn't have the people skills necessary for their new position. Most of us have worked for good technical people who couldn't manage an ant farm. Our traditional beliefs are that they will learn these skills with more experience. This does not necessarily occur. Too often, the manager who possesses only minimal people skills either doesn't recognize the need or concentrates on his or her technical skills to make up for it. This just doesn't work.

This is not only a lesson about our traditional organizations, it is a call to reality for project managers. Often project managers are selected to lead projects because of their technical skills or knowledge. They may go into a critical project without the people skills they will need to be successful. Technical skills and people skills are not the same. In fact, in many ways they tend to be at opposite ends of the skill spectrum. Technical skills tend to be focused and detailed. Management skills are more interactive, communicative, and motivative. A successful project manager must have both sets of skills. He or she must be technically competent, at the level the project demands, and people competent to lead and work within the project team and resources to attain a successful and timely completion of the project. People skills, therefore, are important skills for a successful project manager.

FACTORS THAT INFLUENCE SUCCESS OR FAILURE

Realistically, there is an infinite list of what can go wrong. The point here is to identify the key issues with project management that can enhance or derail one's efforts. Let's talk about nine issues.

Cohesiveness of Project Team. One of the main challenges for any coach of team sports is to build and maintain a cohesive team. These, of course, are two separate activities. Watching Dream Team 2 at the 1996 Summer Olympics®, it was easy to see the importance of a coach's ability to build a team. The team had a surplus of talented players, but from one game to the next you really didn't know which "team" was going to show up. In some games they would work together and blow the other team away. But in other games, and often against less skillful foes, they would struggle to find their rhythm and then squeak out a narrow victory because of the individual efforts of one or two players. Building a cohesive team is not easy but it is essential to a team effort—in sports or in project management.

The other challenge is maintaining that team dynamic. Professional basketball teams are especially susceptible to this challenge. The season of a professional basketball team lasts 82 games. That's a long time to remain cohesive. Similarly, projects can be laborious, long, and demanding. Keeping team cohesion, especially during the uphill portions of the project, is essential to project success.

Project Culture of the Organization. An organization's project culture is developed over time by the history of success or failure, and by the influence of upper management. How does the organization's culture influence the treatment of projects? It can be positive or negative toward project proposals. It can be supportive of projects or abandon them. It can provide resources or not. It can give one-time approval or require ongoing approval. It can be second-guessing and micro-managing. It can expect success or failure. It can champion successful leaders or ignore them. It can adopt one approved and blessed project management method or leave it up to each project manager's choice. It can be extremely formal or casual. It can celebrate challenge, problem solving, and learned solutions or it can shoot the messenger. It can build a team of people and learn from them or it can destroy teams and ignore their input. The project culture of an organization can tremendously empower or limit the success of a project.

Project Tools and Methods Used. It's no grand revelation that some project management tools and methods work well and others don't. Furthermore, some project management tools and methods merge into an organization's personality, philosophies, and management concepts well and others are a mismatch. So this issue isn't just about choosing the best tools and methods for project management and standardizing them in the organization; it is also about making sure that the tools and methods chosen weave into and compliment the organization.

Achieving this is a two-phase effort—first, choosing the tools that best fit an organization's culture, and second, standardizing the process that works across the organization. This is of such significance that Chapter 6 is devoted to it.

Commitment of Proper Resources. Some organizations try to "cheap-out" when it comes to committing resources to a project. It is commonly called "living on a shoe string." Without the proper resources, however, it is more like "dying on a shoe string." There are two issues here—finding the best resources for the job and getting those resources to commit to the project.

Few projects can be done entirely by one person, and the bigger the project, the more resources are needed for it to be successful. This correlation is not negotiable. Keep in mind that not all resources are created equal. Some are good, some are great; others are a complete waste of time and money. The unfortunate disconnection is that sponsoring management often doesn't understand these two facts. Because of this, they tend to put the project on a "shoe string" budget to encourage fiscal responsibility. Is this a flaw in management? No, it is a flaw in information. Management didn't understand the importance of proper resources because no one took the time to inform them of the cause-and-effect relationships. Make no mistake about it, committing proper resources is of critical importance to a successful project. Knowing this, it is the responsibility of the successful project manager to carry the necessary information to sponsoring management.

Sufficient Budget and Time. In our everyday lives, having enough budget and time seems like a luxury. In project management, however, they are essentials. The two problems associated with budget and time are defining what is a "sufficient" amount of each and knowing that sponsoring management must authorize both.

The first problem, knowing what "sufficient" means, is a function of good project planning. Effective project management specifies what a project will cost and how much time it should take. Aside from any temptation to add "contingency time," calculating sufficient budget and time issues directly from a properly managed effort.

The second problem is more complex. It is rare that sponsoring management provides excess budget and time. The majority of the time, the allotment of these resources is too little. This may be the result of tight fiscal resources, customer demands or promises, or routine management practice. Whatever the reason, if insufficient time and budget is allocated to a project, it has an uphill battle to fight. If the constraints are too tight, the project can only fail. It will be doomed to be locked into a predictable cycle of delays and cost overrun approvals.

Micromanagement. As the name implies, micromanagement seeks infinite detail and clarity. This type of management is often locked in semi-decisionmaking or individual decisionmaking concerning each detail in a project's life. It is not a one-way street, though. Because it is a detailed and constant assault, it usually requires detailed and constant attention as well from the project manager. In other words, dealing with micromanagement takes over the project manager's time, rather than working toward the completion of the project. This is not an efficient or successful way to manage a project. In fact, micromanagement not only slows and delays projects, it can also be the project's death knell.

Trying to Do It All Yourself. Ever play volleyball on a team with a "ball hog"? A lot of fun, wasn't it? Chances are your team lost, too. The constant "Mine" or "I'll get it" is an open statement that the team-thing just isn't working. Trying to do it all yourself is rarely a successful strategy. A project manager who says "This is *my* project" or "I'll get it done myself" has the same dismal chances of success as the volleyball team with an unrelenting ball hog.

Successful projects require team commitment and effort. Team effort is the direct result of the project manager's orchestration of the project effort. Orchestration is very different from solo performance. Just as the word implies, many different instruments are directed in such a way as to make beautiful music. One person playing all the instruments is not only inefficient and impractical; it is impossible. In project management, you can't do it all yourself.

Communication. Metaphorically speaking, if the project is going from one place to another, communication is the vehicle taking it there. This is an important perspective because communication is not just critical in project management; without communication, you have no vehicle at all in which to make progress. There is, of course, both good and poor communication. To continue the metaphor, poor communication could be thought of as driving an old, mechanically challenged car as your only means of transportation. Good communication, in comparison, is like taking a jet airplane instead. Communication, therefore, is not only necessary for the coordination and speed of a project, it is also the means for arriving at the destination at all.

Sufficient Skills. We've talked about the many skills that a project manager needs to be effective. They include project management skills, team skills, communication skills, and people skills. There is a rule I've stated many times: "Training must precede expectation." To be successful and effective project managers, we must build the necessary skills for success. We must learn and hone our project management skills. Choosing a method we think is effective is not enough. We need to become proficient in it. We need to think in its terms. We must become skilled in team building and working effectively in teams. In all of these efforts, we need to become better skilled in communication. None of these skills are natural. Many are contrary to what we've learned in our upbringing, but communication is the blood of project management that brings all of the skills together. Without communication, the project dies. So we must learn to become skilled in working with and communicating with people.

People skills in themselves are not complex. We simply have to look through the eyes of others to see how best to meet their needs. Too often, we only look through our own eyes. We focus on the urgency of our own problems rather than the problems of those on whom we depend. This is a 180 degree difference in perspective. We need to put these people skills into action because they are critical to successful project management.

Key Issues of Project Management

• Cohesiveness of Project Team
• Project Culture of the Organization
• Project Tools and Methods Used
• Commitment of Proper Resources
• Sufficient Budget and Time
• Micromanagement
• Trying to Do It All Yourself
• Communication
• Sufficient Skills

OVERVIEW OF PHASES AND STEPS

Within this book, I introduce a method for project management. I wish I could say that this method was the product of my own creativity. The truth is, however, that it is not. It is, instead, the product of many years of learning, reading, initiating, observing, and managing projects. It was not derived from one great and wise source but was compiled from many sources over many years. Many authors claim that they have the one and only pathway to success. The notion is that if you put your faith in any method it will work. To me, this is foolishness. My focus has never been on merely working though any method. I am more of a perfectionist. I don't want a method to merely work or be durable. I want it to be the best, most efficient, most effective, and most successful method available.

This is where my many years of exposure to projects and project management pay off. The method enclosed in this book is an aggregate of ideas that have metamorphosed over many years, with many influences placed layer on layer. Schematically, it looks like the project management model seen in the figure on the next page.

This is a three-phased approach to project management: Concept and Approval, Planning and Analysis, and Project Implementation. Like the project itself, each phase has starting and stopping points that define the phase's scope.

Phase I begins with the initial project concept, moves through expansion of the concept, on to identifying what the project will accomplish and what risks are inherent in the project, then to fully identifying all project objectives and constraints toward obtaining a preliminary project approval. This is a check-in point that assures minimal wasted time should this preliminary work not produce a project approved for funding. It also serves as a springboard for developing the project picture or map—a detailed identification of the project's tasks and jobs and their sequence. Further, the resources necessary to accomplish the tasks and jobs are identified and quantified. The termination point of this phase is the go-ahead approval, which begins the serious and costly project work. This go-ahead approval is made from a point of near total knowledge of the project's objectives, schedule, costs, and resource requirements.

PROJECT MANAGEMENT – PHASES AND STAGES

Phase I: Concept and Approvals

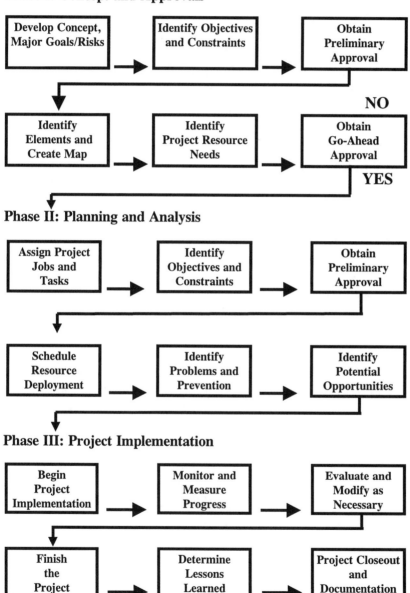

| Develop Concept, Major Goals/Risks | → | Identify Objectives and Constraints | → | Obtain Preliminary Approval |

| Identify Elements and Create Map | → | Identify Project Resource Needs | → | Obtain Go-Ahead Approval |

NO

YES

Phase II: Planning and Analysis

| Assign Project Jobs and Tasks | → | Identify Objectives and Constraints | → | Obtain Preliminary Approval |

| Schedule Resource Deployment | → | Identify Problems and Prevention | → | Identify Potential Opportunities |

Phase III: Project Implementation

| Begin Project Implementation | → | Monitor and Measure Progress | → | Evaluate and Modify as Necessary |

| Finish the Project | → | Determine Lessons Learned | → | Project Closeout and Documentation |

Phase II is the planning and analysis stage of the project. This is where the meat is placed on the bones, or project map. Assign who is going to be responsible for each task or job. Identify a critical sequence. This critical sequence is the heartbeat of the project and must be accomplished in order and on time if the project is to be delivered on time. Develop a graphical display of the total project. Many graphing methods can be used but the Gantt chart is probably the most widely accepted for this purpose. Resources are scheduled against the time sequence of project tasks. Finally, project analysis is done—look for potential problems that can slow or stop the project and for proactive preventive actions that become part of the project plan. Potential opportunities to gain support or hasten the time are identified. These become key focus areas just in case the project finds rough waters.

Phase III is the actual project implementation. This is the phase of dirt-moving, foundation pouring, detailed drafting and design work, developing the table of contents, and contracted work on the project. This phase is orchestrated by the project plan and schedule. Monitoring and measuring systems are utilized to keep track of the progress and pulse of the project. As expected or unexpected occurrences are confronted, the plan, schedule, or resource deployment is modified. This monitoring, measuring, and modifying continues until the project is complete. But even after completion, this phase is not finished. It should also include a detailed team dissection of the project, looking for lessons that can be learned and not repeated. The final step of this phase is closing the project and making sure that everything is documented.

From the beginning of the project concept to close-out and documentation, this three-phase, eighteen-step process for managing projects assures that nothing is forgotten or goes unconsidered. Following this standardized process, the failure rate, over-budget project rate, and the missed on-time project delivery rate can all be greatly reduced.

SUMMARY

Thank goodness project management is not brain surgery or nuclear physics! It is instead a step-by-step process that can be used universally for successfully managing projects. To be successful, however, some specific skills are required. It requires a successful project manager with project management skills, team skills, communication skills, and people skills. The last three skills are particularly important because effectively accomplishing projects is not a solo activity. Even the most skilled project manager with a superior project knowledge of management processes will fail most of the time if he or she does not realize that project management is a team leadership, coordination, orchestration, communication, and partnershipping effort. The better the project manager's skills are in these three areas, the more likely the project will succeed and unexpected problems will be minimal.

3

PHASE I: CONCEPT AND APPROVALS

The engineering manager of a Fortune 100 company came to an established environmental engineer and gave him the challenge of his career. "There is this production facility that considerably contaminated from over thirty years of operation. We are beginning to get hints from regulatory agencies that we should be putting together a cleanup plan. This isn't an easy job. It's complex, and could take years, many years to complete, but it will have high upper-management visibility. Do you want it?" The engineer thought to himself, "Careers are built on projects like this," and said, "You bet I want it." After the rush subsided, he started thinking, "What the hell do they really want to do with that facility?" This was a premonition.

How do you clarify a foggy or wishful project concept? After all, what does "putting together a cleanup plan" really mean? Some initial project concepts aren't even that clear. You might get something like, "Let's improve it" or "If we doubled the rate" or "If we could cut the exposure rate in half." These aren't project concepts. They are dreams and aspirations. There is a big difference! But the truth is that initial project concepts seldom provide a clear picture of what you are supposed to do. Rarely do you get, "We want the X-process rebuilt in area 12 to include the new Z applications by next November." An experienced project manager would fall off his or her chair! This level of clarity of initial project concept may be the case in 1 out of 1,000 projects. More often, you are faced with an unknown project (if it exists at all technologically) with an uncertain placement and an

57

uncertain time for completion. So, for a successful project manager, one of the first and largest challenges is to clarify the project concept.

In our example, the experienced environmental engineer spent the next three years trying to bring clarity to this project's concept. Upper management really wanted the whole facility to just go away, become invisible. They had no interest in doing anything they weren't forced to do, and then only to the minimum involvement necessary, with the least cost. The company's lawyers really didn't want to put anything in writing or to make the first move. Lawyers like someone else to make the first move. That way, they can be smart in how they respond to it. The regulatory agencies weren't anxious to tell them what to do or if anything needed to be done. They didn't want the responsibility for the decision if history or public opinion should determine that they were wrong.

Nor was the Fortune 100 company anxious to ask the regulatory agencies to take a stand. Factually, the company was dead set against asking. The facility's management just wanted to be left alone. They were only interested in making their next quarter's production and profit numbers and really didn't want any expenses, especially large ones, added to their overhead. The corporation's environmental group was so tied up in internal politics, they were literally unable to make any decision. They would be of no help at all. What the environmental engineer had was a "can of worms"—a huge, smelly, wiggling, unstable can of worms. This was something quite different from what he had expected. It was something that careers can be unmade by.

STEP 1: IDENTIFY PROJECT CONCEPT, MAJOR GOALS AND RISKS

In college basketball, you can play a man-on-man or zone defense. One of the most traditional zone defenses is called the "box and one." It is a zone defense consisting of a strong box defense played by four of the five players. The coach determines the fifth player's role. It can be to stay man-on-man with the best offensive player, stay and guard the post, or roam the baseline. The strength of the "box and one" defense

PROJECT MANAGEMENT – PHASES AND STAGES

Phase I: Concept and Approvals

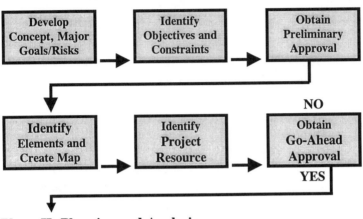

Phase II: Planning and Analysis

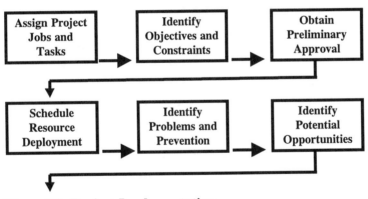

Phase III: Project Implementation

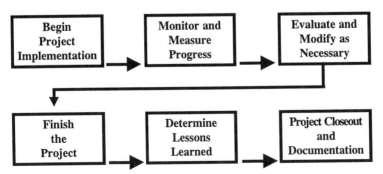

is the box and the use of the one other player to focus on a specific potential problem that the offensive team presents.

This is a very good analogy of Phase I of project management. The box represents the four elements of the project's concept that must be in place and in agreement. These four elements often are referred to as the project definition. The element outside the box represents a special effort focused on risks the project has the potential to present.

The four elements of the project's concept are results, budget, time, and value. They must be present if a project is to have any clarity and purpose. These form the boilerplate for a successful project.

Results. What is the end product of the project? Is it a new process, a new piece of equipment, a remodeled building, a cleaned environmental site, a completed safety manual, a compliant chemical safety program, a new local exhaust ventilation system, a reorganized department, a flattened organizational structure, a higher level of employee participation, etc.? The final product of a project is the result.

There are a couple of dangers here. First, we sometimes think that we get extra points from management if we embellish the written description of the result. For example, "The final result will be a local exhaust ventilation system with at least 200,000 scfm, a heated and air-conditioned make-up area that removes the toxic exposures at any place in the work zone (20'x20') to below the 8-hour TLV, STEL, and Ceiling levels." Wow, this sure sounds more impressive than, "Install a local exhaust ventilation system." But, remember that the purpose of the result is to focus the project, not impress management. Simple and straightforward is always best when defining a project result. Don't include any more detail than is absolutely necessary to define what the end product will be.

Second, sometimes we are tempted to describe the desired outcome of the project as the result it is supposed to accomplish. For example, we may be creating and implementing a chemical safety program. A misdefinition of our result might say, "Eliminate any possibility of a chemical overexposure or accident." This is the desired outcome of putting in to effect a chemical safety program. It is *not* the result of the project. The result, instead, is simply, "To implement a chemical safety program." There should be no flowers in a project result statement. It should be simple and to the point. The question one should ask after writing the project result is, "Does it clearly and simply define what is to be done so I know when the project has been completed?" This is important because if you should decide halfway throught the project that your flowery result is not accurate because of the details, you may never get an "All-Done" from management or your boss.

Budget. What is the project going to cost? This can be firm or open-ended. For example, if your management said that they have $100,000 available for your project, simply stating that the project will stay within the $100,000 budget is fine. If, however, the project is so new or complex that no one knows what the cost will be, it's okay to state, "within a budget to be approved by management."

A budgetary statement is critical in project design because it defines an important border. It says to management, you have control here, not "the sky's the limit." This is an important point to take into account when seeking preliminary or final approval for the project. Management gives these approvals based on the budget and the project manager must feel comfortable that he or she can manage the costs of the project. This is why specifying a budgetary limitation is critical to a project definition.

Time. A project definition must have a time limitation or goal. When is the project to be completed? Many projects don't have a completion date, and as a result, they never get done. The purpose of a project is to complete it, *not* to work on it. Taiichi Ohno, the father of Just-in-Time manufacturing (commonly called the Toyota Process) talked about this important distinction. He made the point that two commonly used Japanese characters are confused.

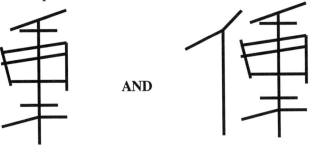

Both of these characters are pronounced the same (doe). The character at the left means "to move." The one at the right has an additional element that literally means "person." Adding this element changes the meaning. Together they mean "to work." Ohno's point is that too often we think we are employed "to move" or be busy, when actually we are employed "to work," meaning to actually accomplish something.

This is also a point about project management and why the time element is always included in a successful project definition. The purpose of any project is to get it done. A time limit helps us focus on when it needs to be wrapped up. Not having a definite time limitation or goal, the urgency to get the project moving and keep it on schedule becomes lost. We simply strive "to move" the project along, not "to work" the project to completion.

Value. If a project is worth doing, worth spending money on, worth the time, worth committing resources to, it must bring value to the organization. In other words, doing the project has to represent an improvement in something that contributes to the success of the organization. Too often, we get caught in the trap of doing projects because someone high up had the idea or because it will keep people busy or because we have money available. The federal government finds itself in this trap very often. It forgets that its project efforts must add value.

The question we must ask in our project definition step is "So what?" "What is going to be different when the project is complete? Is something going to be better, more productive, safer, healthier, of higher quality? Will it save money, increase revenue, make workers happier and more productive? What is going to be improved *and* is that improvement big enough to justify the costs, time, and resources project completion will demand?" This is a *big* question and one that shouldn't be taken lightly!

Also keep in mind that the answer to the question of whether the project has value makes a difference. Answering, "No, not really" isn't just an exercise in truth. If the answer is "No," "Maybe," "I don't know," "Only marginal," it is cause to **Stop!** More pointedly, it may be a good enough reason to kill the project. This is a gate question. It must pass this gate affirmatively or common sense should tell us to stop. If it doesn't, something is wrong with the decisionmaking process or with our values.

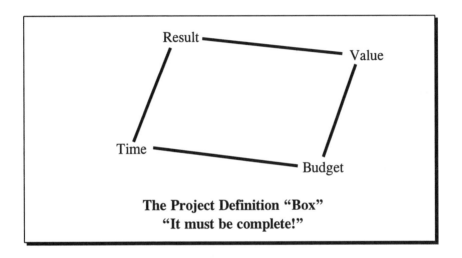

The Project Definition "Box"
"It must be complete!"

Risks. Completing the project definition box leaves us with one more element—defining the major project risks. There is an emphasis on the word "major." This is not a search for everything and anything that could conceivably delay, cause problems, frustrate, and impede communications. Rather, this a search for "show stoppers." "What risks are inherent in or with the project that could blow the project, or the reasons for doing it, to pieces?" Some obvious areas to search include the following:

- Is the technology going to work or is there sufficient technology already developed?
- Will we infringe on any patents?
- Are there available resources to get the project done?
- Will we create an even larger safety or health concern?

- Is there something out there that can totally derail the project?
- Is there required permitting or licensing that could delay, change, or derail the project?
- Are there any major upper management paradigms or insecurities that can delay or complicate the project?
- What kind of extra costs or cost increases could blow the budget?
- Is there anyone or any resource that, if not available or on time, could delay the project?

The result of Step One is to develop the statement of the project into a clear, simple format. The project statement tells what will be accomplished, when it will be done and with what budgetary constraints (if any). For example:

> *Move the Safety & Industrial Hygiene office and laboratory to the new building by March 16 for under $2,000.*

There is a real temptation to get too flowery and add objectives to the statement. That must be avoided. For example, adding *"from building 102 across town to 156 E. Filmore Street"* is too much detail. Additionally, adding *"with minimal or no customer interruption"* is really an objective and shouldn't be included in the project statement. It is also important to know that the project statement is not a stand-alone item. It exists *with* the project objectives and constraints. Together they become the complete project description.

The project statement is a critical starting point in project management. If this is done poorly or incompletely, the entire project has a strong probability of being fatally flawed. The "box" must be completed. The results, budget, time, and value of the project must be determined, and the project statement must be written and clearly stated. The major risks of the project need to be determined. In attempting to get a clear project statement, find true value to the organization, and analyze the major risks, a project manager can make the decision whether to proceed or stop.

DUFFY

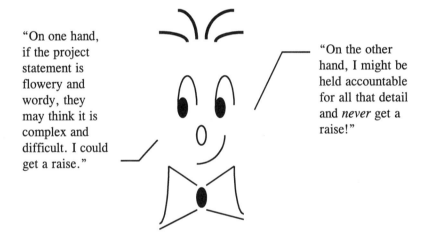

"On one hand, if the project statement is flowery and wordy, they may think it is complex and difficult. I could get a raise."

"On the other hand, I might be held accountable for all that detail and *never* get a raise!"

STEP 2: IDENTIFY PROJECT OBJECTIVES AND CONSTRAINTS

Every project has objectives. Once completed, the project must accomplish or satisfy these objectives. Objectives answer the question, "Why are we doing this?" Or, "When the project is complete, what will be the benefits?" Objectives focus the planning to remind everyone, including the sponsors, what benefit all this work and money will ultimately provide to the organization.

Objectives must be quantifiable; that is, you must be able to identify whether or not you have accomplished them when the project comes on-line. They can be measured either by degree (such as "improvement by 10%") or pass or fail. Objectives such as "To make the process safer" cannot work because they are not measurable. Objectives need to be specific and describable.

Examples of Project Objectives

- This project will lower the 8-hour TWA to less than 50% of the PEL.

- This project will increase production 25%.

- Completion of this project will decrease quality errors 5%.

- When finished, cycle-time for the XYZ production will be decreased 10%.

Objectives are accomplishments or benefits of the project that are important enough to write down to assure their completion or attainment. They are not the project result itself. *Objectives are statements that can only be realized because of the result via project completion.* Writing them down keeps them in focus throughout the entire project. After all, they are that important—they are the reason the project was launched in the first place.

Project constraints are those inherent obstacles, resistances, limitations, or considerations that must be included in a successful project map. They may require allocation of resources, planning elements, extra approvals, extra communication, etc. But they are "deal with" elements, not "eliminate" issues. You cannot level every hill or remove every roadblock, and project constraints are a normal feature of the terrain. You have to admit their existence, make them visible by listing them, and deal with them in your project planning. Examples of constraints include statements like these:

Examples of Project Constraints

- Complete sub-project #1 by July 15 when the lease runs out.

- Use only unionized labor in the contract.

- Meet the Vice President's desire to have the office relocation done before June 20, the end of her vacation.

- Have the permitting accomplished by October 31.

- Meet the building code requirements for Area 66.

- Coordinate all aspects of the project using a contract team.

- Communicate the completed milestones via the employee newsletter.

The purpose of a separate step to list project objectives and constraints is the visibility it offers. You can't manage something if it is invisible. Listing objectives (the "benefits of the project") and constraints (the "need to deal with aspects of the project") helps the project manager and his or her project team identify the important elements of the project during the planning process. It also allows sponsoring and approving management to know why the project approval was warranted, and to see that all constraints, including their concerns and needs, are being considered and included in the project planning.

Before a successful project manager rushes to obtain the preliminary approval, the project statement, list of major risks, and the list of objectives and constraints need to be shared informally with sponsors and customers to check for agreement and completion. This is an important action because it identifies missing elements or misunderstandings *before* the open review of the preliminary approval process. It has another advantage in that it gives each sponsor and customer information so they aren't surprised or tempted to dissect the preliminary approval presentation. More importantly, it gives everybody involved early ownership of the project. This advantage will provide dividends later in the project's life.

There are some notable pitfalls to making a list of objectives and constraints that can be easily avoided if known.

Pitfall #1: Making nonmeasurable objectives. After you've listed your project objectives, double-check each to make sure they are measurable.

Pitfall #2: Some objectives, if achieved, could be due to other causes. If these kinds of objectives are made, you can't claim success if some other cause is, or might be, responsible. Likewise, if something else directly causes the objective to be accomplished without your influence, you've failed.

Pitfall #3: Making the objectives too "Big Picture" rather than "low post." It is natural for us to want to "free the world," so we tend to make our objectives larger than life. In managing a project, however, this is not the time for overly ambitious, outside-realm objectives.

Pitfall #4: Measures of accomplishment that are too complex, subjective, or time-consuming. Complex and subjective measures only lead to argument. You say you did it, but others, possibly sponsors or your boss, could say that you didn't. Also keep in mind that the most important thing is to successfully accomplish the project, *not* to spend all your time measuring objectives. Make measurement simple and easy.

Pitfall #5: Stating objectives that add no benefit or value to the project is also dangerous. Don't get caught in the ego-correlation, "the more objectives I list, the more important my project will be" trap. Make only the objectives that are critical to your project. If your project is only supported by "fluff" objectives, someone will ask the terrible question, "Why are we doing this?"

Pitfall #6: Not gaining or testing understanding from customers, sponsors, or stakeholders. Gaining understanding is a function of the all-important communication responsibilities of a successful project manager. It is too important to assume things are understood and not check for understanding.

Objective and Constraint Pitfalls

- Making non-measurable objectives

- Making objectives that, if achieved, could be due to other causes

- Making the objectives too Big Picture

- Making the measures too complex, subjective, or time-consuming

- Making objectives that add no benefit or value to the project

---

STEP 3: OBTAIN PRELIMINARY APPROVAL FOR THE PROJECT

Preliminary approval is the first formal check-in with sponsoring management. The initial consultation focused on project concept, but a lot of work has been done since then to define the project, identify the major risks involved, and document the project objectives and constraints. Now it is "show time."

Trying to get preliminary approval is not as simple as throwing a folder of project information on your boss's desk and waiting for a blessing. It is much more complex than that. Seeking preliminary project approval is more like courtship. First impressions mean a lot. The form and content of the communication is critical. So is the packaging of the information. And knowing when and how to ask for approval is a matter of timing and opportunity.

To this end, there are some simple rules for seeking and obtaining preliminary project approval.

Rule #1: Package the information appropriately and effectively. The information must answer questions, not generate them. It must also be of sufficient detail without being too detailed. It also needs to be factual, realistic, and attainable. The information needs to be functionally packaged, error proof, and pleasing in its appearance.

Rule #2: Know who needs to see the information and what kind of lead time they require. Everybody in the organization or management chain may need to have access to this information. Sponsoring management may also require that someone else see it—an expert in your organization, perhaps. The best advice here is to ask who needs to see what when.

Rule #3: Request face-to-face presentations or meetings that meet the project's urgency. Even if you are in a hurry to get started, your urgency doesn't translate if the project is of lesser importance to sponsoring management.

Rule #4: Use the appropriate method for answering questions and requesting approvals. Every project does not require two-hour formal presentation packages or slide shows. Some projects do, but most do not.

Rule #5: Know when it is *not the time* to ask for approvals. Sometimes it is much wiser to back off rather than rush into a forced decision. If a project is worth doing, the process of seeking and obtaining preliminary approval must also be done correctly.

Rules for Seeking and Obtaining Approval

- Package the information appropriately and effectively.

- Know who needs the information and what lead-time is required.

- Request meetings or presentations that meet the project's urgency.

- Use the appropriate methods of answering questions and requesting approvals.

- Know when it is *not the time* to ask for approval.

Make sure that all the relevant information is presented to sponsoring management. This information starts with a complete project definition—result, budget, time, and value. It includes major risks that may confront the project and a complete documentation of the project's objectives. This is critical because a sponsor must know why he or she is authorizing the project. How will it benefit the organization? And, finally, the information must specify the constraints under which the project must be conducted.

Preliminary and final approvals always come with some "conditions." There tend to more conditions in preliminary approval stages because the more substantial detailed information isn't available yet. Generally, these conditions come from the natural questioning process. Why is this project important? How firm is the time and budget? What kind of resources are anticipated? Are these all of the risks? What is the project payback in terms of objectives? Have the project concepts been thoroughly thought out? Would changes now provide greater benefits later? These sorts of questions are the origins of placing conditions on the preliminary approval.

Factually, the number and severity of the conditions really come from a project manager's answers to these questions. More exactly, conditions will arise if there is a lack of answers. This means two things to a successful project manager—do your homework and produce a complete information packet for management! The correlation looks like this. **#1:** Not having the right or a sufficient amount of information in the information available for sponsoring management means a greater number of questions. **#2:** The greater the number of questions, the greater the probability of your not knowing or not having the right answers. And, **#3:** The more questions that come up without satisfactory answers, the greater the number and severity of conditions will be attached to the preliminary approval.

What kind of reasonable conditions can you expect? Reasonable conditions may include a preliminary budget until more detailed information is available, regular check-in's with sponsoring management; regular status reports to sponsors; designation of a liaison through which critical information and project status can flow; or a second proposal in which you need to have more details to present. You will routinely deal with one or more of these reasonable conditions in even the best-managed projects. But you can expect that the greater the budget or time needed, or the higher the priority of the project to the organization, the greater the number of the conditions will result.

STEP 4: IDENTIFY THE MAJOR PROJECT ELEMENTS AND CREATE A PROJECT MAP

Chances are that in your determination of appropriate budget and time, you've already developed a rough list of what needs to be done. This rough list identifies the major project elements. Let's use an example from childhood that most of us are very familiar with. Say you want to build a snowman. A list of the major project elements or deliverables might look like this:

Project: Build a Snowman

- Begin the project.

- Select a site for construction.

- Chose a design for the snowman.

- Build the snowman.

- Find and install the desired snowman decorations.

- Project completion.

This is a step-by-step breakdown of the project from start to finish. It is important that every project have an actual "begin" step and an "end" step. This is just good practice and it assures that everyone can identify when the project is started and when it is completed.

The development of the project map is the step in the process where the details or tasks are added to the major project element skeleton. When completed, this is commonly called a task breakdown.

Developing a complete and accurate task breakdown is critical to successful project management. This step must be done completely and done well. If you miss important steps, all of your decisions and actions past this point will be flawed. The identification of necessary resources can come up short. The estimation of time and budget can also be off course. This critical step must be done carefully, and it must be reviewed, revised, corrected, and added to until it is complete. This is one area where the team aspects of project planning can have a definite advantage. In a team-planned project, there is much less chance that items, especially critical or costly items, will be missed. A more detailed task breakdown of our snowman building might look like this:

Project: Build a Snowman

1. Begin the project.
   A. Get permission to build a snowman.
   B. Wait for a snowy day.
   C. Make sure the snow has excellent pack-ability.

2. Select a site for construction.
   A. Make sure there is enough unused snow for your snowman.
   B. Secure permission to use this site.

3. Chose a design for the snowman.
   A. Make sure there is enough snow available for design.
   B. Make sure design allows for lifting lighter loads on base loads.

4. Build the snowman.
   A. Roll the base snowman ball and put in place.
   B. Roll the second snowman ball and lift into place.
   C. Roll the snowman head and lift into place.
   D. Pack sufficient snow around joints to secure placement.

5. Find and install the desired snowman decorations.
   A. Find and install branches for arms.
   B. Find and install small rocks for nose, eyes, and buttons.
   C. Find and install a hat and a scarf.

6. Project completion.

Creating a project task breakdown doesn't require reams of paper or expensive computer programs. One simple technique is to use 3M Post-It® Notes or their generic equivalent. As new deliverables or tasks are identified, these "stickies" can be easily moved around on a desktop, a wall, a poster board or other uncluttered work surface. Using this technique, team brainstorming can easily and effectively be used to create a very thorough task breakdown.

Let's look at a safety and health example of a project called "Installation of Anodic Ventilation System." First, we will develop a list of major project elements.

Project: Installation of Anodic Ventilation System

1. Begin Project

2. Quantify Evolution Rate

3. Design Ventilation System

4. Install Ventilation System

5. Monitor Employee Exposures

6. Project Completed

From this list of major project elements, we can construct a task breakdown to complete the project. We will use a simple grid worksheet for clarity.

Project: Installation of Anodic Ventilation System

Tasks			
1. Begin Project			
2. Quantify Evolution Rate			
A. Conduct Area Monitoring			
B. Get Results of Monitoring			
C. Calculate Evolution Rate			
3. Design Ventilation System			
A. Determine Design Specifications			
B. Determine Inlet Design/Placement			
C. Select Appropriate Fan			
D. Design Electrical System			
E. Design Ducting System			
F. Design Ventilation Discharge			
G. Acquire Complete Drawings			
4. Install Ventilation System			
A. Put Design Out for Bid			
B. Select Ventilation Contractor			
C. Award Contract			
D. Contractor to Install as Designed			
5. Monitor Employee Exposures			
A. Perform Monitoring			
B. Calculate Exposures from Results			
6. Project Completed.			

There are other project mapping techniques that can be used. The one used in these examples is a vertical breakdown of tasks. Another two-dimensional method that is commonly used is called process mapping. This technique is a horizontal breakdown that places all tasks in individual boxes and connects the boxes in the appropriate sequence with arrows. This technique is especially advantageous when a task is followed by concurrent tasks because multitask relationships can be difficult to display clearly in a vertical task breakdown. The following is a horizontal task breakdown of a portion of the previously used anodic ventilation system example. In order to show the clarity with which this technique can display multitask relationships, only project major element 3, Design Ventilation System, is used in this task breakdown.

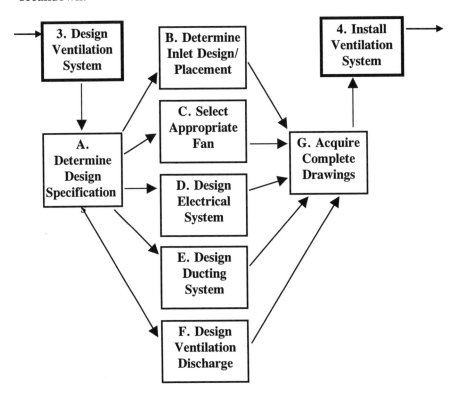

Task Breakdown Using Process Mapping Technique

The vertical breakdown technique is far better for continuing the planning process. The grid or spreadsheet format is ideal for information expansion and for clarity in defining and identifying the steps that follow. It allows a project manager to capture all the information on one spreadsheet page. By far, this is the best way to keep all issues, needs, and responsibilities visible and manageable. On the other hand, the horizontal mapping, two-dimensional technique adds visual clarity to the sequence and concurrence of tasks that the vertical technique just can't. This is extremely valuable when identifying responsibilities and resources assuring that none overlap or are overtaxed during any project period. It is valuable in helping the project team visualize the critical task sequence and as a visual prop to share with sponsoring management in seeking approvals.

There is a danger in having too many major project elements. The general rule is to have no more than eight major elements. If a project has, say, 16 or 18 major elements, it generally needs to be broken down into separate but linked projects. Having more than eight major elements is most often too much to effectively accomplish.

Task Duration: There is one more piece of information required in this step. Each task needs to be given duration: How long will it take to do? This is important for accurately determining how long the project will take to accomplish. For this purpose, both the vertical task breakdown (or grid) and the horizontal breakdown (or process map) have distinctive advantages. The vertical task breakdown allows an easy identification of how long each task will take. Let's apply task duration to our example.

Project: Installation of Anodic Ventilation System

Tasks	Duration		
1. Begin Project			
2. Quantify Evolution Rate			
A. Conduct Area Monitoring	1 day		
B. Get Results of Monitoring	2 weeks		
C. Calculate Evolution Rate	2 hours		
3. Design Ventilation System			
A. Determine Design Specifications	1 day		
B. Determine Inlet Design/Placement	2 days		
C. Select Appropriate Fan	1 day		
D. Design Electrical System	2 days		
E. Design Ducting System	1 day		
F. Design Ventilation Discharge	1 day		
G. Acquire Complete Drawings	2 weeks		
4. Install Ventilation System			
A. Put Design Out for Bid	2 weeks		
B. Select Ventilation Contractor	1 day		
C. Award Contract	3 days		
D. Contractor to Install as Designed	90 days		
5. Monitor Employee Exposures			
A. Perform Monitoring	1 day		
B. Calculate Exposures from Results	2 hours		
6. Project Completed.			

Clarity of sequence is the advantage that the process mapping technique provides. Obviously, some tasks can be done simultaneously. This is best displayed using the horizontal mapping technique. Also, using this technique in determining task duration shows which time durations add to the total project length and which ones do not. For example, using the third major project element, specifying duration, would look like this.

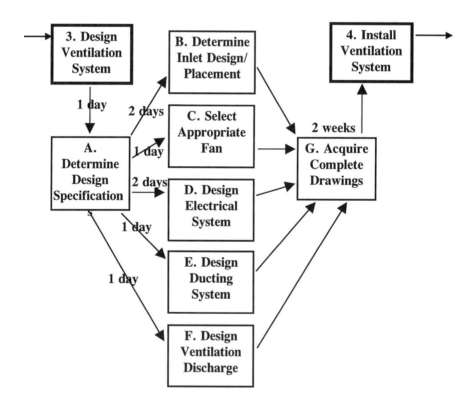

Using this technique, it is clear that tasks 3B through 3F can be accomplished concurrently—provided sufficient resources, of course.

This time relationship is not as easily determined using the vertical task breakdown technique. Viewing the vertical task breakdown, it would appear that the major element would require 18 days to complete. The horizontal display shows clearly that this major element would require only 13 days because of the concurrent nature of some of the tasks.

STEP 5: IDENTIFY PROJECT RESOURCE NEEDS

This is the "who does what?" and "what do we need?" step in the sequence. One person seldom accomplishes projects single-handedly. Required resources tend to expand with the complexity and size of the project. These resources fall into several areas.

People Resources. These include those people inside the organization, those outside the organization, or those who service the organizations, such as corporate staff who are involved in the project. These people can be grouped by function or specialty—such as purchasing, engineering, drafting, contracting, or safety and environmental.

Equipment Resources. These resources do not include hammers, moving dollies, or other generic equipment that are common to the facility. Equipment resources include those specialized or limited availability pieces of equipment that must be scheduled, coordinated, purchased, leased, or contracted out. These include specialty survey equipment that is not part of a facility's industrial hygiene lab, cranes for lifting or moving equipment, moving trucks, etc.

Contract Resources. These include those specialty functions that will have to be purchased. These include construction, demolition, ventilation design specialists, ergonomists, environmental remediation or engineering firms, lion tamers, drafting support, etc. Anyone or any service that must be contracted needs to be noted.

Power Resources. These refer to internal politics. If any task requires internal power to push it through, get needed support, or authorize changes or communication, those power resources need to be noted.

The vertical task breakdown is ideal for identifying needed resources for each task. It is difficult, however, without the benefit of adding a lot of side wording and confusion to use the horizontal mapping technique. A grid is normally used for the task breakdown because the next column can be reserved for resource identification. Using our anodic ventilation example, identifying resource needs appears very differently using the vertical and horizontal mapping techniques.

Project: Installation of Anodic Ventilation System

Tasks	Duration	Resources	
1. Begin Project			
2. Quantify Evolution Rate			
A. Conduct Area Monitoring	1 day	Industrial Hygiene	
B. Get Results of Monitoring	2 weeks	Industrial Hygiene	
C. Calculate Evolution Rate	2 hours	Engineering	
3. Design Ventilation System			
A. Determine Design Specifications	1 day	Engineering	
B. Determine Inlet Design/Placement	2 days	Engineering	
C. Select Appropriate Fan	1 day	Engineering	
D. Design Electrical System	2 days	Electrical Engineering	
E. Design Ducting System	1 day	Engineering	

F. Design Ventilation Discharge	1 day	Engineering	
G. Acquire Complete Drawings	2 weeks	Drafting	
4. Install Ventilation System			
A. Put Design Out for Bid	2 weeks	Purchasing	
B. Select Ventilation Contractor	1 day	Engineering	
C. Award Contract	3 days	Purchasing	
D. Contractor to Install as Designed	90 days	Contractor	
5. Monitor Employee Exposures			
A. Perform Monitoring	1 day	Industrial Hygiene	
B. Calculate Exposures from Results	2 hours	Industrial Hygiene	
6. Project Completed.			

As you can see by examining the chart on the next page, the clarity of information is much better using the vertical technique. Additionally, this lack of display clarity of the horizontal mapping technique is more confusing when more resources are used.

Color-coding can also be used to identify which resources are needed with each task. This approach, of course, is restricted to those having color capabilities and is limited by the number of colors that are easily identifiable. In very large jobs needing many different resources, this limitation can be a large obstacle.

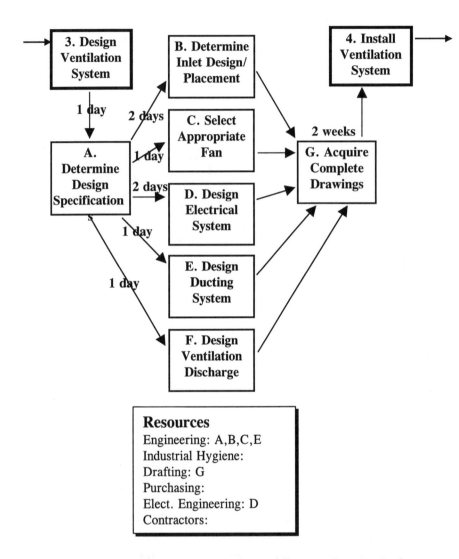

Resource Identification Using Process Mapping Technique

STEP 6: OBTAIN GO-AHEAD APPROVAL FOR PROJECT

Obviously go-ahead approval is an important step in the progress of a project. It is the "live or die" step. The specific difference between efforts to obtain preliminary and go-ahead approvals is based on eminence. Seeking a preliminary approval, you are going in with only an analyzed project concept. Since the details are not presented yet, the information available to sponsoring management is incomplete. This leaves too much room for open-ended questions. It is the first time that the sponsoring management has had a chance to view the project past the initial rough concept phase. The project hasn't had the time to invite management anxiety, detailed thought, and input from everyone else in the organization. There is little risk of making a bad decision in giving a preliminary approval. Management is going to see it again in more detail after a lot of thought and analysis has been put into it. Preliminary approval doesn't risk a lot of time or money.

Obviously, the issues associated with a go-ahead approval are much different. The stakes are much higher to management and to the organization. This is a "put your money and the resources where your mouth is" step. This is the step for commitment. Now there is a complete project plan to review, analyze through different eyes, and comment on. In the go-ahead approval process, unlike the preliminary approval process, the detailed information present in a well-planned project increases the chance of hard questions. The project manager, however, is more knowledgeable and able to answer these tougher questions.

There are five necessary outcomes of this go-ahead approval for the project manager. The successful project manager must have all the elements in place to arrive at this point. These five essential elements are budget, resources, time, sponsorship, and contract.

Budget. You cannot buy a car for $10. You cannot build a house for $1,000. Likewise, you cannot successfully manage a project without an adequate budget. The key word here, of course, is "adequate." A traditional saying goes, "You get what you pay for." If you try to cut costs too closely or just do not commit to the necessary funding, you cannot expect to get what you want. Unfortunately, adequate funds are rarely committed to a project.

Why does this happen? Largely due to three reasons: First, it may be considered a function of management to ask for miracles. Give 90 percent of what is necessary and challenge the project manager to find ways to get 100 percent of the project done. This is usually a long-standing component of a management culture. Second, the organization's culture may be one that habitually underfunds projects and then reviews for additional budget. It's called "low-balling." And third, the project manager may simply ask for too little. This is usually a function of not planning adequately or having additional costs thrown in during the go-ahead approval process.

Obviously, there is commonly some sparring and negotiating that occurs between sponsoring management and the project manager. Often management makes sure that the project manager is prepared and did his or her homework. It's a form of "Prove it to me." There are also many times during this budgetary negotiation that parts of the project will be scrapped or delayed. The approval step may be the first time that sponsoring management has had a look at all the costs, and the first time the project manager has known the real budgetary restraints. This is a common communication breakdown. But as negotiations reduce or expand parts of the project, it is done in plain sight of all—the project manager and sponsoring management. It becomes a negotiated settlement where both parties agree on what "adequate" means and what project elements will or will not be accomplished.

There are also "budget games." These are normally part of the organization's project management culture and are usually perpetuated by the project manager. One game is called "high-balling." Knowing negotiations will lower what he or she asks for and that there will be a management expectation for the project to be completed anyway, the project manager "inflates" the cost estimates. The thought is that ground gained by the inflation can be negotiated away, leaving an adequate budget to accomplish the project.

Both sides of these negotiations are called upon to make commitments in reaching a budgetary agreement. Sponsoring management commits to the project, and promises that the funds will be available when needed. The project manager commits to living within that agreed-upon amount. Too often, however, this is not the case. One side may enter the agreement with little commitment to abide by the settlement. After all, it's rationalized, we really don't know what the future will bring and we can always go back and ask for more. But this agreement should, in fact, be a matter of integrity. If you make the agreement, live with it—do what you say you are going to do. Don't wink at the importance and the commitment required of a negotiated settlement.

Resources. When pyramids were being built with forced labor, human resources were a simple issue. The bigger the project, the more labor it took. They'd just go out and round up more labor, depending on the need. In today's world of paid labor, human resources can literally cost more than the equipment or facilities. Completed design drawings and process and instrument drawings (P&IDs) can easily cost $2,000 per finalized sheet. If a project requires 100 to 200 drawings, it is easy to calculate that the cost would be $200,000 to $400,000 for drawings. This doesn't take into account engineering costs if outside resources are required. A large mobile crane can easily cost $2,000 a day. But all of these resources are critical if the project is to be accomplished. Resource needs must be included in the project plan, made visible with the costs to sponsoring management, and made part of the approval process. The amount of money allocated to needed resources can become an issue to sponsoring management if, for some reason, some resource costs are missed in the approval-seeking process. This fact can derail a project all together, should it occur.

Time. Time is another area where there can be wide differences between the project plan and the desires of sponsoring management. Management wants the project to be completed RIGHT NOW! Projects don't work that way. They take time. The more complex or larger a project is, the more time it usually takes. This seems obvious but it isn't always so to sponsoring management. "It will take *how long*? Oh, that's just too long." This is where the skill of the project manager becomes extremely important. The project manager needs to negotiate timetables so that he or she has sufficient time to complete the project and so that sponsoring management gets something back in return, less the time.

Obviously, there is temptation to stretch the time requested so that it can be negotiated back. This is another "game" that is too common. Like playing "budget games," it is an integrity issue.

But at some point in this negotiation process, reality must creep in. The pyramids weren't built in a weekend, nor can you accomplish a project in less time than needed. It is critical that you know precisely what your time limitations are when seeking the go-ahead approval.

Sponsorship. A project manager does not have authority over all aspects of the project's implementation. This authority can only be gained through sponsorship. Because of this, it is important to get a sponsor assigned to the project and to make sure the sponsor is right for the specific project. The right sponsor has authority over the necessary project resources or has direct influence with those that do (e.g., via upper management team).

Sponsorship assignment also assures project visibility and a single point for communication with appropriate levels in management. These are not small advantages to a project manager. Much time can be wasted communicating with too many people when a sponsor will be more efficient and effective.

There are, after all, three sources of power critical to accomplishing a project. The first source is *legitimate power*. This is power that is given from above. In project management, it is usually assigned to the project leader. This power, however, is not enough. The second source of power is *basic power*. This comes from several areas. It comes from knowledge, skills, and other personal attributes that a successful project manager must have. But, more important for our focus, it comes from the project's sponsorship position in the organization. This power can *only* be acquired via sponsorship. The last source of power, as Covey tells us, is *interpersonal power*. This is much more esoteric and harder to define than the other forms of power, but it is critical to successfully accomplishing a project.

Contract: I'm not referring to a written form of a contract but a verbal one. It is a contract between the approving management and the project manager that all issues have been resolved, and that each will live with what has been agreed upon. This verbal contract is the foundation of trust for the project. It is based on factual communication, truthful representation, honest negotiations, commitment, and integrity. The integrity of the project manager will be tested by how he or she sticks to what was agreed upon throughout the project. If the project manager's integrity is an issue or is suspect going into these approvals, all bets are off—reaching this all-important verbal contract can be all but a dream.

Obviously, there are three possible outcomes of seeking a go-ahead approval. 1) You can get the approval and move on to Phase II of project management. 2) Management can send you back for more information. Normally, this sends the project manager back a couple of steps into Phase I. 3) The project can be derailed. Although rare past the preliminary approval step, derailing of a project can and does happen. After having successfully navigated the discovery of Phase I, it can be a tremendous letdown for a committed project manager. But it is an outcome that a project manager must be prepared to deal with.

"THINGS THAT GO BUMP IN THE NIGHT"—THE FOUR BIGGEST PROBLEMS IN PROJECT MANAGEMENT

There is a Cornish prayer, attributed to that prolific writer, Anon. In it we find some useful philosophy: "From ghoulies and ghosties and long-legged beasties and things that go bump in the night, Good Lord, deliver us!" The prayer emphasizes our fear of the unknown, of what is out there in the dark. The philosophical lesson for us today is that a simple action can remove this fear—*turn on the lights*! The ancient Cornish did not have this convenience. So perhaps, after discussing the steps in Phase I of project management, it is a proper time to turn on the lights and point out the four biggest and most often encountered problems in project management.

The first problem, *projects that never end*, has been talked about before. It has its roots right here in Phase I. A project that is never given a clear end point—the project statement—continues to evolve, grow, and expand, but never end. A project *must* have a clear and agreed upon, written, formalized, known to everyone end point past which it becomes a new and different project.

The second biggest problem in project management, *having no clear project and agreed upon objectives*, occurs when the project itself is amorphous and undefined. Perhaps, for instance, we simply want to "improve" something, or we want to "review and construct if necessary." In these cases, what is the project? In fact, no one really knows. Likewise, not having project objectives that everyone agrees on is death to the reputation of a project manager. Say, for instance, that Sponsor #1 thought that the project had to raise production by 10 percent, while Sponsor #2 was convinced that a quality goal of improving first-time-through production by 2 percent was the objective. If you don't accomplish both, to one of them you are seen as a bum. This problem is rooted in Phase I.

The third biggest problem in project management is *having resources that are not really committed*. Having this commitment should be one of the go-ahead approval goals. Often, however, sponsors give only partial approval or unspoken disapproval, especially in the area of committing resources. To prevent this from happening, the added responsibility of the successful project manager is to check for potential roadblocks to resource commitment *prior* to the go-ahead approval presentation, double check for approval *during* the go-ahead approval step, and personally contact all sponsors *after* the go-ahead approval is given to confirm their commitment. If they don't take these steps, the cost is too heavy for a project manager later.

The fourth biggest problem in project management is *making too many assumptions*. In reality, there is NO place for ANY assumptions in successful project management. Don't assume what someone knows. Don't assume that the status or progress of the project is clear. Don't assume that people are sharing information. In other words, don't assume anything. If you do, there is a very high probability that your assumption will be incorrect.

SUMMARY

Phase I: Concept and Approvals

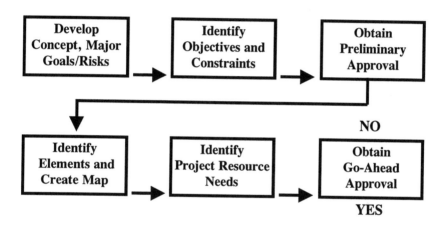

Phase I of project management is comprised of six interrelated steps that begin with the initial project concept and end with the go-ahead approval from sponsoring management. It is a phase filled with analysis and discovery. It is the phase where a rough, often idealistic, project concept is developed into a defined, realistic, and workable plan. It is a phase in which a project moves from being mysterious and dreamy to being known and identifiable. It moves from the shadows of the organization to the daylight of committed emphasis. It moves from guesses and estimates to negotiated and approved numbers and time.

4

PHASE II: PLANNING AND ANALYSIS

After the completion of Phase I, it can be a confusing time in the life of a project. Having the go-ahead approval from sponsoring management, a firm idea of what the project will accomplish, agreement and commitment of budget, resources and time, it seems to be the right time to just get on with it! But wait! At this point, you really only have half of the deck. This isn't a time for project implementation; this is a time for even more intricate planning and discovery. Phase II makes it possible to stay within the budget and to complete the project on time, which is key for a successful project manager.

The purpose of Phase I was really to gather enough details about the project to get it blessed. Phase II is the ultimate planning and discovery phase of the program. This is where all the tasks are arranged into an orchestrated effort and where all potential roadblocks and opportunities are revealed, explored, and planned. You should not miss this important phase or move ahead too quickly—discovery happens as the wolves come to the door. It's better to plan so the wolves can be avoided in the first place.

A large environmental remediation project was begun, headed by a well-known, national, experienced environmental consulting firm. There was considerable pressure placed on the project management to move the remediation along as quickly as possible to minimize regulatory attention, added costs, and micromanagement.

PROJECT MANAGEMENT – PHASES AND STAGES

Phase I: Concept and Approvals

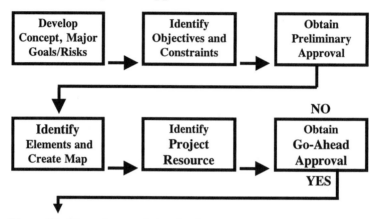

Phase II: Planning and Analysis

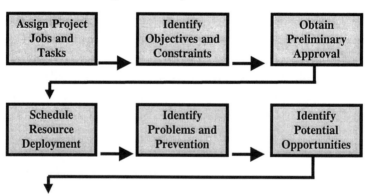

Phase III: Project Implementation

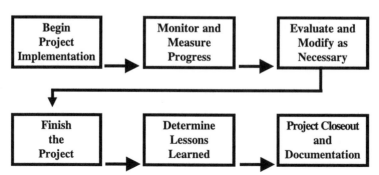

The property under remediation was sloped and seemed to have more than its share of surface water running through it when the weather turned wet. From previous experience, the amount of running surface water was a large concern to the environmental consulting firm. The customer agreed that the storm water needed to be captured and treated prior to discharge off-site. Trailer mounted collection tanks, or frac tanks, were found and brought to the site. A runoff barrier was quickly constructed and a low corner of the facility was modified to serve as a temporary runoff collection pond. When it would rain, water would collect in the low area of the property. Crews would pump the contaminated water into the frac tanks for eventual decontamination. The consulting firm went to work deciding what decontamination method would make the most sense and be the most cost-efficient. Because the contamination was petroleum-based, an activated charcoal system was chosen.

Unfortunately, finding an activated charcoal system of sufficient size was very difficult. The search was being done in the early spring, and that time of year was also a problem. A wetter-than-normal season was confounding the whole situation. In fact, it wasn't just a little wetter, it was double the anticipated rainfall. More frac tanks were brought in, but they were increasingly difficult to find. Shortly, the property began to look like a drag racing convention with numerous cars parked on the grounds.

An activated charcoal system was finally located and rapid transportation was arranged to transport it to the site. Before it arrived, the temporary collection dike ruptured during a heavy rainstorm, allowing approximately 500,000 gallons of contaminated water to escape into the gutter, down the road, and away from the facility. After that, the EPA showed up and halted the project, making any solution to the immediate problem impossible or at least decontamination of the many full frac tanks on the property a remote possibility.

You could argue that events couldn't get much worse. Contaminated surface water was leaving the property, the company had cornered the market on frac tanks in the region, and the company now stood as a monument to poor planning. The costs had gone through the roof, and that wasn't taking into account forthcoming EPA penalties or what project micromanagement would cost. Unfortunately, things *did* get worse—and that's when the media showed up!

Three years after these events occurred, there were still rented frac tanks at the site. What went wrong? The largest problem was simply that this company was in a hurry to finish the project. They didn't adequately plan or anticipate the potential problems that could turn the project back and drive it into the red. This allowed the situation to escalate.

One time, while I was teaching a course on leadership, I conducted a training session focused on planning and team involvement. It was a simple exercise. The class was divided into three teams. Each team was responsible for creating and producing a team banner. Roles were assigned including company president, vice president, research manager, production manager, procurement, labor, design engineering, and union officials. Each team would compete with the others to see who could produce a team banner in the allotted time.

The task seemed simple enough for the teams and all began planning what they had to do. The instructors, however, were there to add some challenges. As each team progressed through anticipated parts of the project, an instructor would hand someone on the team a card that told of a roadblock that they must manage. Needless to say, as the time went on and the roadblocks were handed out, it became a little tense and anxious for each team. Each team, that is, except for one. That team was going about the whole job very differently.

You see, at the starting bell, two teams immediately jumped up and began with a furry of activity, chatter, and excitement. But the third team gathered their chairs together around a table and quietly, calmly began to talk. As the first two teams scurried around assigning tasks, meeting roadblocks, and reacting, the third team continued to sit and talk. By the time two-thirds of the allotted time had expired, the first two teams were nearing their anxiety threshold—often called panic— while the third team slowly began to implement the project plan. Within two minutes, this team's banner was completed. The first two teams never finished theirs.

What was this third team doing for all that time and did it have any bearing on their being the only team to complete the assignment? In the debriefing we all learned that they had spent the first two-thirds of the allotted time planning the project. Once they knew exactly what they had to do, who would do what and how, what the obstacles were, and what the sequence of tasks looked like, they began. The advantage of their planning was obvious. The other teams didn't plan. They just started, but never finished. To the third team, the time spent planning was time well invested. They successfully completed the project in the time allotted.

STEP 1: ASSIGN PROJECT JOBS AND TASKS

In Phase I, you identified the specific tasks or steps that would be required to accomplish the project. You also identified any special resources that would be required, such as experts, outside consultants or services, or services to be done by specialized departments or functions. The first step in Phase II of project management adds assigning project jobs and tasks to that effort by adding a responsibility to each task. An individual task or responsibility left unassigned will not get done. A task will similarly be left undone if it is not assigned to a team, department, or group. When it comes down to accountability, there isn't any if it isn't individually assigned. That's what Step I of Phase II is all about—making specific individuals accountable for accomplishing specified tasks or jobs in the project.

Is assigning accountability really important to a project manager? I've mentioned that project management is not a solo activity. It takes other team players to be successful. Obviously, the larger or more complex the project, the more involvement will be required of others.

There is a lot of work involved in managing a project. Assigning task responsibility and accountability protects the project manager from having to babysit everyone involved to make sure each job or task is being accomplished. Assigning responsibility is a big advantage for successfully managing a project.

Using our previously developed example of a task breakdown grid, let's see how this assignment might look.

Project: Installation of Anodic Ventilation System

Tasks	Duration	Resources	Assignment
1. Begin Project			
2. Quantify Evolution Rate			B. Smith, Lead
A. Conduct Area Monitoring	1 day	Industrial Hygiene	C. Evans
B. Get Results of Monitoring	2 weeks	Industrial Hygiene	C. Evans
C. Calculate Evolution Rate	2 hours	Engineering	C. Evans
3. Design Ventilation System			R. Johnson, Lead
A. Determine Design Specifications	1 day	Engineering	S. Fredrick
B. Determine Inlet Design/ Placement	2 days	Engineering	W. Taylor
C. Select Appropriate Fan	1 day	Engineering	E. Carpov
D. Design Electrical System	2 days	Elect. Engineering	M. Nelson
E. Design Ducting System	1 day	Engineering	W. Taylor
F. Design Ventilation Discharge	1 day	Engineering	W. Taylor
G. Acquire Complete Drawings	2 weeks	Drafting	F. Stanley
4. Install Ventilation System			C. Holmes, Lead

Tasks	Duration	Resources	Assignment
A. Put Design Out for Bid	2 weeks	Purchasing	B. Davis
B. Select Ventilation Contractor	1 day	Engineering	D. Johnson
C. Award Contract	3 days	Purchasing	D. Johnson
D. Contractor to Install as Designed	90 days	Contractor	(TBD)
5. Monitor Employee Exposures			B. Smith, Lead
A. Perform Monitoring	1 day	Industrial Hygiene	C. Evans
B. Calculate Exposures from Results	2 hours	Industrial Hygiene	C. Evans
6. Project Completed.			

(TBD) = To be determined

From this example, we can see two important facets of project management. First, a project manager's job is difficult enough without adding complexity. It simply makes sense to choose methods and techniques for capturing and displaying information that are simple and leave minimal chance of error. A single-page grid or table works nicely for such a purpose. Having all task information simply displayed in one defined space, easily conveys the information to the project team and helps to avoid confusion. This orientation of information also helps those who have been assigned tasks. It is easy to see where a task falls in the project sequence and who is also responsible for project tasks. Additionally, knowing who has responsibility for the task ahead of and behind yours establishes important communication links to assure that no one gets caught unaware and, thereby, fails in their accountability.

The second facet displayed in the example is the different levels of assignment. Every assignment is not hands-on. Each major project stage, such as "Install Ventilation System," is assigned a lead individual. Normally, it is the manager or supervisor who oversees that particular specialty or function. However, a member of the project team can be assigned the duty to communicate with and "bird dog" the task to assure it gets accomplished. Using a vertical task breakdown technique that identifies and separates major phases ahead of the individual tasks makes this "lead" assignment convenient and clear. A major job of this assigned lead person is communication. He or she is responsible for maintaining communication prior to the major project phase, both during and after. This assigned communicator is critical to efficient project flow throughout the sequence of tasks.

These designated lead individuals can be members of the core project team, serve in specialty support teams to the core team, or be independent of any project team involvement. Where they fit is more determined by what project team organization makes sense in the organization, the complexity or size of the project, or the wishes of upper management.

STEP 2: ESTABLISH A CRITICAL SEQUENCE OF TASKS AND DEPENDENT TASKS

The critical sequence of tasks is the string of dependent tasks that if broken, delayed, or failed at any point, will cause delay of the project. The tag "critical" refers to their importance in completing the project on time. They are not necessarily the most complex tasks, nor do they demand the greatest resources. Each task in the critical sequence is merely locked to those ahead and behind it. For example, you cannot submit an environmental permit before it is written, edited, revised, and approved by management. Submitting the permit is independent (by time sequence) of training area management or human resources on the elements included in the permit application.

Every technique has its Achilles heel. This is where the vertical task technique struggles or fails. The vertical task technique does not work well for identifying or displaying critical sequences. The process mapping or horizontal task technique is better suited for this purpose.

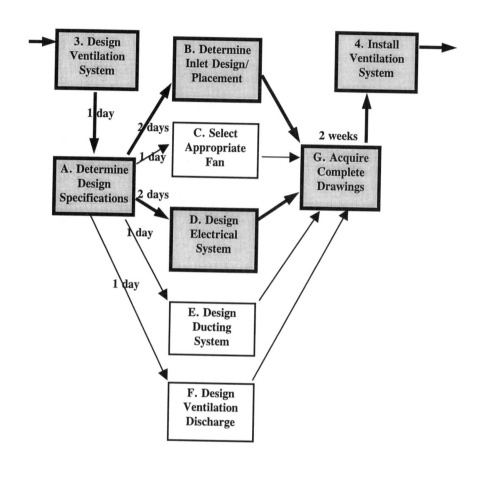

Determining Critical Sequence Using Process Mapping Technique

Using this technique for displaying the overall task sequence, it is easy to identify the critical sequence through all the concurrent activities and to highlight them (see shaded area), which adds clarity for the project team, key project players, leads, and sponsors.

Identifying a critical sequence informs the project manager what tasks require special attention so that they are accomplished within the scheduled time. Tasks that appear later in the critical sequence become "dependent" upon every task in the sequence before them. Their schedule and on-time accomplishment depends on those previous critical tasks. Noncritical tasks, or those that are outside the critical task sequence, can be given some "room" to slide without delaying other tasks in the critical sequence and the project length

DUFFY

"I tried to explain the critical task sequence to my Controller. He spent a lot of time saying 'Uh-huh' and looking out the window. Then he asked why I needed the money..."

"I guess next time I'll use crayon on poster board. That'll make it a lot easier for both of us."

This critical task relationship is like a relay race in track and field. The focus is on the baton, *not* the runners. It is the baton (the project) that must travel from start to finish. Obviously, the only way it will make it there is to be carried by runners (the task-doers). The first runner starts the race carrying the baton toward the second runner. The second runner cannot advance until the baton arrives. At that point, the baton can be handed off to the next runner to be carried the next distance. This sequence dependency continues until the last runner, running the anchor leg, crosses the finish line with the baton. If the baton is dropped anywhere along the way, the runner has to stop and retrieve it before continuing. If the runner fails, gets injured, or slows, every runner after him or her in the race sequence is delayed, as is the total race (project) time. It therefore becomes critical that the distance run by each runner, like each task of a project, be accomplished in the best possible time in order for the race to be won.

Because of this dependency, the duration assigned to these critical tasks becomes very important. If too little time is set aside for a task, it delays the end date and every task after it. This delay is very detrimental to scheduling resources, and often very costly. If too much time is given to a critical task, the entire project takes a nap. Because the end line can not be extended, the purpose of successful project management is to be as efficient as possible. Time spent waiting due to time overbudgets to a task is called Q-Time. Time spent waiting is always wasted time. Because time is our only real limited commodity, wastes of time can be frustrating to those involved and to sponsors, especially when dynamic project measurement is used.

Identifying duration also allows a project manager visibility of where task times might be too tight. Tight critical tasks become higher priority management issues as the project moves closer to them. Extra management effort may be required, including adding plenty of pre-task communication time and time for confirmations with resources, time for reviewing schedule requirements for the task, or time for micro-sequencing of the task to assure it is known and well-planned. These tight-time tasks are noted for use in Step 5 of Phase II.

Also, tasks with overbudgeted time must be identified at this step. "Make-up" opportunities may arise and these are noted for use in Step 6 of this phase.

STEP 3: DEVELOP AND CHART PROJECT SCHEDULE

With each step, more meat is added to the bones—the task breakdown. In actuality, the project schedule has already been developed and used for determining critical and dependent tasks. Step 3 is a refinement step where the project schedule is charted and finalized. Charting, like exploration maps, is a visible, fairly accurate depiction of the project's course. Set up in a calendar format, the chart becomes a day planner, the visible day-to-day schedule of the project. To this point, time has been relative to each task as task duration. The sequence was merely a function of tasks or jobs. The charting of a project in Step 3 makes these same tasks and jobs a function of time. This is an important distinction. Up to this point, our plan was a do-this-and-then-that sequence. Charting this same sequence makes the project time-specific. In reality, we work by time, not task. If we work by task, time becomes a secondary variable. But if we work by time, duration becomes the primary focus.

Charting is normally done on a left-to-right calendar grid with the task breakdown identified top-to-bottom on the left margin. Two different charting representations or functions are used. Tasks identified as major project phases (e.g., 3. Design Ventilation System) are highlighted on the chart. The actual tasks that have been assigned time durations are displayed using a different means, usually lines or boxes that cover the day or days in sequence.

Using the anodic ventilation example, the major project phases have been shown using a heavy line with a downward arrow to mark the beginning and the end. Individual tasks are shown using a narrower line without beginning and ending arrows. There is no standardized method of charting, although many different methods have been used. The purpose isn't to standardize but to differentiate between tasks and show their relationship to time.

Project: Installation of Anodic Ventilation System

Tasks	Duration
1. Begin Project	
2. Quantify Evolution Rate	
A. Conduct Monitoring	1 day
B. Get Results	2 weeks
C. Calculate Evolution	2 hours
3. Design Ventilation	
A. Design Specifications	1 day
B. Determine Inlet	2 days
C. Select Fan	1 day
D. Design Electrical	2 days
E. Design Ducting	1 day
F. Design Discharge	1 day
G. Acquire Drawings	2 weeks
4. Install Ventilation System	
A. Design Out for Bid	2 weeks
B. Select Contractor	1 day
C. Award Contract	3 days
D. Contractor to Install	90 days

5. Monitor Exposures		
A. Perform Monitoring	1 day	
B. Calculate Exposures	2 hours	
6. Project Completed.		

(TBD) = To be determined

The process mapping technique or horizontal task technique can also be used to chart project information.

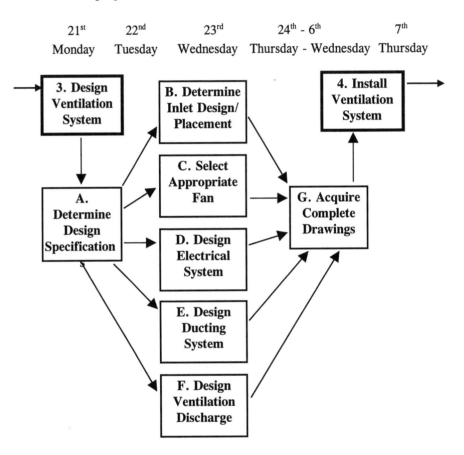

21st	22nd	23rd	24th - 6th	7th
Monday	Tuesday	Wednesday	Thursday - Wednesday	Thursday

Using this horizontal technique, no lines or other methods for showing duration are required. The left-to-right sequence of the tasks automatically shows this relationship with time.

It is important that the critical sequence or path be distinguished from noncritical tasks. In the vertical task chart, this is often done by color or by using a different pattern of black or gray lines. In the horizontal charting, this can be done simply by highlighting the boxes and connecting arrows. Making the critical sequence of tasks stand out assures that they are not lost in all the other information. Remember that this is project plan development. With every step, the project becomes more defined, more planned, and potentially more confusing. Care must be exercised to retain clarity of the information. It is important that visual clarity be added to keep the critical sequence easily identifiable in all the expanding information of the project plan.

The developed project chart is an important step in the planning of a project because it will drive the management of the project implementation from beginning to end. This should not be a half-hearted effort. The project chart is very important because it provides sequence, schedule, calendar, and interrelationship.

One of the most popular charting methods is the Gantt chart. Basically, the horizontal task chart shown in our example depicts a Gantt chart. However, the Gantt chart is much more standardized in form and legend usage. Standardization helps to avoid confusion between one person and another, especially between the project manager and his or her sponsors, and between project team members.

It is also obvious to see that as the information expands, it is best if it can all be kept in one format. The horizontal task breakdown doesn't have a common row or column, and therefore information becomes pooled or jumbled and easily confusing. The vertical task breakdown, or Gantt, on the other hand, is nearly ideal for this purpose. The only restriction, of course, is how wide the paper is that is used to capture the information. Obviously, this is an opportunity for computerized or spreadsheet applications. Some project management firms, such as Kepner-Tregoe® have developed project management pads of paper where information is copied onto lower sheets using carbonless paper technology. The pad of information becomes the project plan, capturing all information relative to each sheet's focus or purpose. I will discuss more on this project management tool in Chapter 5.

STEP 4: SCHEDULE RESOURCE DEPLOYMENT

The resources needed to accomplish the project were identified in Step 5 of Phase I of project management. A list was developed and attached to the task breakdown. Step 4 of Phase II seeks to plug the resources into the time sequence. Having developed a project chart that displays the task relationship with time, each resource tied to the tasks can now also be affixed in time. For example: the crane is needed on March 23-27. The electrical engineer needs to be available to develop the electrical requirements and drawing by the week of February 11.

Each resource has its own continuum and appears on the chart at one or more places. But those are task accomplishments. In order to affix the task to a time sequence, there are a lot of pre-task and post-task responsibilities of both the project management team and the resource.

Planning Discussion: The project chart/plan is not a mushroom. It is a dynamic tool that will guide the entire project. It must continually see the light of day. As the plan and chart—time line—is being developed, the resources will have input on the schedule. For instance, there may be only one ventilation engineer and he or she is tied up on another project that week. Or travel may be involved, making pre-planning and more detailed scheduling necessary. These discussions test the metal of the plan and schedule. Probing questions by both the project management team and the human resources at this time is critical. "When do you mean?" "Do you want us on-site or ready to roll this day?" "Are you sure nothing else may delay your dedicating people?" This is another location of verbal contracting, but this time the verbal contract is a commitment between the project management team and the human resources.

Plan Sharing: Once the plan has been *set* (the plan is a dynamic tool, it really never gets *finalized*), it needs to be shared with all human resources and team members. This is the Big Picture review. "What comes before my task?" "What comes after?" "Who is the oversight person for this major project phase?" "Are there any potential problems or overutilizations of resources?" Overutilization is a major potential derailing force for a project manager. This Big Picture review, when all tasks and resources are looked at, offers an opportunity to count up the hours committed, the days required, and assure that no one is working a 32-hour day.

Pre-Task Communications: It is the responsibility of the project management team to assure that adequate pre-task communication is accomplished. No one likes to be kept in the dark and suddenly have the curtain go up. This lack of communication is not only a problem for the human resource but it could also blow up in the face of the project manager. Adequate means just that—you don't need to schedule daily calls to make sure your human resources are tucked in, but the frequency of communication should definitely increase the closer it gets to the scheduled task.

One cannot assume that any one communication pathway is best for everyone. Because we are all individuals and have differing schedules, home bases, and support structures, our communication pathways are also different. These differences need to be determined so that pre-task communication can be accomplished without assumption—that is without, "I assumed you got the message."

Post-Task Close Out: This is the first time we see the lessons-learned aspect of project management. Each human resource deployment is a mini-project. From those experiences there are always things to learn: Was the communication sufficient? Was there enough lead-time? Was enough time given to the task? How effective was the communication and coordination between others involved in the project? Where can the process be improved next time?

Post-task close out also includes billings and payments, etc., for outside or contracted resources. This is not solely the responsibility of the Accounts Payable Department; it is a continuation of the communication responsibilities of the project management team.

STEP 5: IDENTIFY POTENTIAL PROBLEMS AND MAKE PREVENTION PLANS

Generally speaking, the plan for project implementation can be considered complete in Step 4. So, what else is there to do? Have you ever had a project, or anything else that had to be run on a schedule, that didn't hit some unexpected snag along the way? Most of us would have to answer no to that question. We seem to always run into unexpected obstacles. Things often go sour at the least opportune time. That's why Steps 5 and 6 are included in the project management process. They are the contingency and opportunity planning steps that can literally make or break project deadlines.

Where in a project process can the wheels come off? For example, what happens if the crane doesn't arrive on the Thursday? Or what happens if our electrical engineer is sick the week he is scheduled to work on this project? What happens if management can't make a decision about a resource deployment during a critical sequence task? Step 5 seeks to ask the hard questions, the ones no one really wants to think about. But, by asking these questions, we also strive to find ways of preventing the project from derailing or being severely delayed.

The following is a sequence of questions that can best be used for this purpose.

Question #1: What tasks, critical or noncritical, require the most resources or are the most complex?

Question #2: What task durations are the tightest?

Question #3: What tasks are critical to more than one dependent task downstream?

Question #4: What tasks are accomplished by resources totally outside the project manager's or project management team's control or influence?

Question #5: What tasks are most likely to get pushed tighter by management or by the assigned resources?

Question #6: What tasks are assigned to resources that, in the past, have been less than dependable?

Question #7: What tasks are assigned to resources that are (or appear to be) overbooked or overworked?

Question #8: What tasks are led by members of management or of the project management team who are less dependable, overly committed, or too busy?

These questions point out those tasks that can potentially derail a project.

Which of these questions are the most important ones to ask? Which ones require a project manager's complete and focused attention? The answer is simply "All of them." This may seem overwhelming, but it is merely a call for contingency planning.

An engineer with a large manufacturing plant was once assigned leadership responsibilities for a major upgrade project. That upgrade in the production process would require a new product pathway, which meant a two-week shutdown during Christmas time. The engineer was an experienced project manager so he planned all of the details of the project. In the project go-ahead approval presentation, a particular task in the project process that required a crane for moving major equipment hit a snag.

The snag centered on the question of whether it would be best to rent a crane or use the facility's large mobile crane. The project manager knew that many other projects would have to be accomplished in the same timeframe and that many of them would need the mobile crane's services. In talking with other project managers, he felt the existing crane would be overtaxed and not dependable for such a critical project like his. As a result, he strongly recommended renting another crane. Because the rental of the crane was going to cost a bundle for the one day it was needed, they hit a snag. No decision could be made and time was lost in waiting. The project manager was instructed to reconsider using the facility's mobile crane, and was presented an additional schedule of its use during the shutdown week before a decision could be made.

His reconsideration found that, during the 16-day shutdown, the mobile crane was uncommitted on days 1, 2, 7, 13, 15, and 16. The other days the mobile crane would be busy for more than two-thirds of each day at some other location within the facility, far from the site where he needed it. Days 1 and 2, however, were too early in the project for use of the crane, and days 13, 15, and 16 were too late. That left the engineer with one possible day—day 7. But that day wasn't ideal because it was two days before the crane-needed task was scheduled. Somehow, though, management didn't understand the difficulty of the situation and denied his request for rental of an outside crane.

Wanting to be successful regardless of the decision, the project manager set about modifying the project task sequence so that the facility's mobile crane could be used on the day it was available. With great difficulty, he found a way to schedule the crane on day 7. He forgot, however, to do any contingency planning. It turned out that the mobile crane was delayed one day on a previous task, pushing all of the following tasks back a day. That time could be made up, the engineer thought, by doing some intelligent retrofitting prior to the machine movement, but this could be tricky. Things didn't get better for him. The mobile crane was needed for other purposes an extra four hours on the day he needed it (now day 8). By the time the crane had traveled across the plant to his work site, only three hours of an 8-hour workday were left. The project staff worked into the third shift to get the job done. But the retrofitting wasn't correct and required an additional shift to correct. By now, the engineer was over budget and at least a day behind. "Over budget" and "behind" are not encouraging words to sponsoring management, a project manager's boss, or the production people who must have the process turned over to them on a particular day.

The project was signed-off and turned over to production two days late. The budget overrun and the two-day production loss that required overtime to correct would easily have paid for the crane rental. But it wasn't the project manager's fault—or was it? It seems that it was the fault of the sponsoring management in not making a good decision, doesn't it? Wrong on both counts. It really *was* the engineer's fault. He had done no contingency planning so any effort at "crunch time" was unplanned and chancy. Furthermore, if there was a significant probability of project delays and costs involved, he needed to let sponsoring management know when the go-ahead decisions were being made. Management doesn't have a crystal ball. They are also rarely out to get anybody. They make the best decisions they can at the time they need to make them with the amount of information and options they are given. The engineer gave them a "take it or leave it" decision without any contingency or what-if cost analysis, and they left it.

As a friend likes to put it, identifying potential problems is a "witch hunt." Face it, regardless of how simple the project is or how human and other resources are or aren't involved, somewhere in the sequence of tasks, you are going to hit a snag. Nothing is so well planned that unexpected things don't happen. Snags will happen, period! Knowing this, it doesn't make any sense to manage a project without prevention planning.

In reality, this step has three parts—identifying the potential tasks that can cause problems, determining what could cause each problem (the root or underlying cause), and developing a prevention and correction plan for each identified task. Did I say each identified task? Yes, I did. No identified task is less or more important than the others. If each task can cause problems to a project's budget or timetable, it is important. It is common, however, to deal with only the most important ones. We do, after all, deal with finite resources—especially time. So, assigning probability to each problem is often helpful to target efforts. Additionally, identifying the severity of a potential problem can also be very helpful. Obviously, those problems having a high probability of occurrence and a high severity of consequences are critical need areas for prevention planning. These problems are followed by those having a lower probability and high severity; then by high probability and low severity; and finally by low probability and low severity. In reality, large, complex projects with many low probability and low severity problems can be moved to the "fly by the seat of your pants" department.

Severity of Problem

Probability Problem Will Occur	High Probability High Severity	High Probability Low Severity
	Low Probability High Severity	Low Probability Low Severity

What preventive strategies can be used? Sometimes, increased communication and status information can effectively minimize potential problems. Other potential problems may require more extensive preventive measures. These could include contingency contracting; identifying makeshift onsite resources that can be used if there are no other choices; assigning dual oversight roles; increasing check-in or written status reports; talking directly to those resource people who will do the job without going through the management chain (with approval, of course); creative scheduling; or doing it yourself (always the last option).

Corrective plans, then, are those plans made before the problem actually occurs. They minimize the damage when it does happen. But with corrective plans, it's important to identify triggers in potential problem tasks. These triggers are points in the corrective plan where corrective actions are automatically implemented. A trigger can happen before the task is scheduled—such as when a resource tells you that your job has been "moved out"—or it may happen when the first day of a three-day task is missed. Triggers automatically implement corrective actions without rationalization and with minimal decisionmaking.

Identifying potential problem areas and planning prevention for them is a "make or break" step in project management. Problems will occur. Often the difference between a highly successful project manager and one who has the reputation of being marginal is based on how well they achieve this step. So, it isn't just a "make or break" step for the project, it is also a test for the success and reputation of the project manager.

STEP 6: IDENTIFY POTENTIAL OPPORTUNITIES FOR MAKING UP GROUND

Step 5 was one of contingency planning—preventing the negative. Step 6 is hero planning—accentuating the positive. These steps are, in fact, opposites that use the same skills. But they are also complementary. In other words, when problems threaten a task, budget, or timetable, where are you going to go to make up ground? As in the lyrics of the theme song to the Bill Murray movie *Ghostbusters*, "Who you gonna call?"

Successfully identifying opportunity tasks can be done in the same way as finding problem tasks. In fact, the same questioning approach can be used, but this time the questions are the opposite.

Question #1: What tasks, critical or noncritical, require the least resources or are the least complex?

Question #2: What task durations are the most liberal (have contingency factors figured in)?

Question #3: What tasks are not critical in a time sequence to other tasks (that can be done ahead of schedule)?

Question #4: What tasks are accomplished by you or by resources that are totally under your control and scheduling?

Question #5: What tasks are most likely to get no attention from sponsoring management or, for that matter, are window dressing and could be forgotten all together?

Question #6: What tasks are assigned to people who have the reputation of getting work done early?

Question #7: What tasks are assigned to people who are underbooked and underworked?

Question #8: What tasks are led by members of management or of the project management team who are always dependable or not too busy?

These questions point to the tasks that can become opportunities for you to make up ground in your project.

Like Step 5, Step 6 has two parts—identifying tasks where opportunities for making up ground might lie, and planning actions to take advantage of those opportunities. These actions might include increasing communication, moving the sequence to take advantage of wasted time spent waiting (Q-Time), requesting more resources from contractors (compacting timelines without increasing overall resource requirements and costs), creating turn-key installations, etc.

A young environmental engineer was assigned a permitting project. The project timetable spanned almost nine months, which was divided into three phases—planning, permit writing, and permit review and approval. The environmental engineering group was responsible for the first phase. The second phase would be done as a cooperative venture between the environmental engineering group and an outside environmental contractor. The third phase was the responsibility of the regulatory agency. There were many critical and dependent tasks in the first two phases. The third phase fell into the hands of the unmanageable, undependable, noncustomer focused, and uncaring regulatory ibis. The engineer identified several critical tasks in the first two phases as potential problems but her major concern was the entire third phase of the project. Knowing that the environmental project really could not begin until approved by the regulatory agency (the third phase completed) a lot rode on completion of the project on time.

The engineer also identified key opportunity tasks. Some lay in the interface between the environmental engineering group and the outside contractor. Mostly, she saw that the third phase, although a high-probability problem area, was also to be an area of opportunity. In order to take advantage of some of these opportunities, she rescheduled some of the tasks. She also added some "task review and stripping" tasks at the front of the project, and exported some of the contractor-provided tasks early instead of when scheduled. This allowed the contractor timeline to be minimized and saved on resource costs—a double payback. She also planned a staged submittal of the environmental permit to the regulatory agency. This was done in person to answer questions and solicit support and was an opportunity for influencing communication. Done in a stage-submitted fashion, many parts of the project could be easily "rubber stamped" as common technology, while others that would require detailed review could be stripped away. This would save a lot of time and questions from the agency. It would also allow the complex permit to be dissected so that sticky points could be visible and easily negotiated or compromised early.

The results of her positively impacting the opportunity tasks were amazing. She completed the project in less than seven months, allowing the project to advance more quickly, seizing important competitive advantages for the company, and saving the company a number of dollars on her project. Now she is a manager of that environmental engineering group.

SUMMARY

Phase II: Planning and Analysis

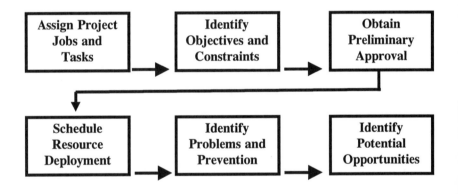

Phase II of project management is the meat of the process. It moves the project past an amorphous structure of definition and go-ahead approval to a filled out structure of a highly known and planned nature. The task breakdown is refined, further defined and detailed, rearranged, and made more efficient. Problems are identified and resolved, and opportunities are planned and taken advantage of. Analogous to the manufacturing of an automobile, Phase I provides a frame sitting on a chassis assembly, suspended by the assembly line's overhead trolley. Phase II adds the interior, the lights and wiring, the motor, the exterior components and the undercarriage parts, the paint, wheels, and tires. Now rolling on its own wheels, engine and all components tested, it is ready for Phase III—rolling off the assembly line to the customer.

There are tremendous temptations throughout Phase II to "just get on with it." What I mean is the feeling that "We've already received the go-ahead approval, let's get the project done!" But just as we can see in our analogy of the car assembly, a frame that is suspended on the assembly line has little chance of running at that point. The customer in Phase III would have little use for this frame as it exited Phase I. So, successful project managers must remain vigilant and committed to the entire sequence of the project management process, knowing that with each successfully completed step his or her chances of overall success are enhanced. Taking shortcuts or not completing Phase II increases the chance of failure and lousy reputation that comes with it.

For many years, I've studied Japanese management. In many ways, that management is an outgrowth of Japanese culture. One of the things I have admired the most is the reverence for patience. This is in contrast to America's seemingly complete lack of patience. Admittedly, a "patience in everything" mindset can be just as bad as an "impatience in everything," but in project management, we can adopt an important quality from the Japanese. Whereas Americans seem to always be in a rush to begin, which can cause planning to be short-sighted, abbreviated or forgotten, the Japanese have a patient approach to it. They recognize that patience and diligence in planning makes the rest of the road easier. This is an important lesson for American business to learn.

Secondly, the Japanese believe in small, everyday improvements as a major source of competitive advantage. Americans, on the other hand, prefer light speed and expensive changes. In America, the word is "Now." In Japan, the word is "Tomorrow." This derives from the Japanese reverence for patience. They express this patient approach to continuous improvement in the word *Kaizen*.

The Japanese have used patience and *Kaizen* very effectively in project management. Much more time is spent in the planning phase of project management than we are used to. When they develop a project plan they massage it, critique it, ask hard questions about it, refine it, tweak it, and play with it, until it evolves into a form that changes little. Only at that point is project implementation begun. What is the reward for such a practice? The Japanese history of successful project completion is without equal elsewhere in the world. Americans historically are less successful. It isn't that our brains are somehow hardwired differently, it is more a societal and business culture issue. Americans tend to spend too little time planning, because there is a rush to get on with it. Consequently, our project implementation tends to have more bugs, problems, upsets, and unsuccessful endings.

Do you want proof? Look at the countless ideas and inventions that American industry has conceived but has been unsuccessful in bringing to completion by successfully introducing them into the marketplace. Consider examples like the flat matrix television screen, fuzzy logic, and compact discs, just to name a few.

We can learn a lesson about patience and *Kaizen* from the Japanese and apply it directly to project management. Patience must always be a part of planning. There must be a reverence for thorough planning, so that project implementation is always a successful continuation of planning momentum. Those who wish to be successful project managers should take note.

5

PHASE III: PROJECT IMPLEMENTATION

"Get ready...get set...GO!" This is the time we've been waiting for. You know, the time when most unsuccessful projects begin—the project implementation phase. Think back over the two phases that we've covered to get here. There has been a lot of work in preparing, communicating, selling, cajoling, creating team dynamics, detailing, negotiating, begging, convincing, presenting, planning, and replanning. These were all accomplished in the first two phases, where the project plan or map was developed. The project implementation phase is the journey that begins to follow the map.

Project Management - Phases and Stages

Phase I: Concept and Approvals

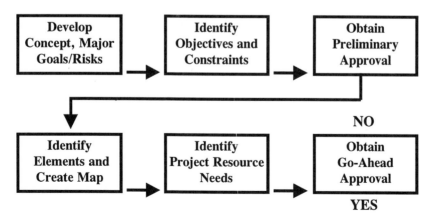

Phase II: Planning and Analysis

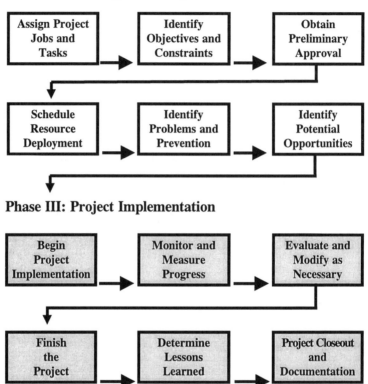

Phase III: Project Implementation

A project was begun that involved construction of a large surface impoundment for holding an aqueous waste stream. Because the waste stream was neutralized prior to discharge and was mostly salt water, there were minimal permitting issues involved. The process, however, allowed very small quantities of naturally occurring radioactive elements to go out in the waste stream. A prudent and foreseeing negotiated agreement with the regulatory agencies provided that the pond be double-lined with leak detection installed between the liners. This was in addition to the already existing perimeter of shallow groundwater sampling wells.

The project had been well planned and many discussions had been held with the involved regulatory agencies to get their input and agreement. The implementation plan was lengthy and detailed. It would take more than seven months to complete the project and would cost over $6 million. Every attempt was made to identify the potential problems and to plan their prevention. This was a well-planned project.

Excavation of the impoundment began. No one around this very rural community had ever seen such large earth-moving equipment. The area became the gathering place for all the locals who just came to watch. That attention attracted the interest of a nearby city's newspaper. A community-interest story was written and published in the Sunday paper that saw wide circulation. That's when an environmental group began checking on permitting for the impoundment—what environmental studies had been filed, and what was eventually going to go in the pond. That was also when the real problems began.

No environmental impact study had been done. The regulatory agency just didn't see the need when the project was first negotiated. However, that opinion began to change. The small rural community residents hadn't been told that low levels of radioactive compounds were being sent into the pond. It didn't matter how small that level was, they became very concerned about their range animals, their well water, and the health of their children.

Meanwhile, the project was continuing on schedule. The arrival and installation of the liner material was quite a production. That's when the question arose: If the radioactive materials that would be released into the pond were so minimal, natural, and "harmless," why would the company spend all that money to double-line the pond and install a leak-detection system? To the environmental group, the community residents, the newspaper, and a growing number in the regulatory agency, that didn't make much sense. That's when a lawsuit was filed to stop the project...and it did. Do you have any idea how much it costs the company to idle a team of large earth-moving equipment and their crews, while simultaneously accruing attorney costs?

DUFFY

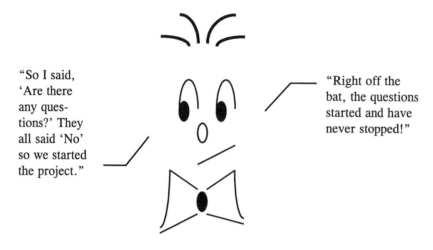

"So I said, 'Are there any questions?' They all said 'No' so we started the project."

"Right off the bat, the questions started and have never stopped!"

STEP 1: BEGIN PROJECT IMPLEMENTATION

In a lot of ways, this seems like a set up. The laid groundwork says that if you plan extensively, get a lot of people involved, and make the effort to develop the project through planning and scheduling, you can't miss. Well, I wish it were always that easy. Most of the time it is. But there are those challenging projects that seem to be destined for trouble.

There are no guarantees in project management. Sometimes it's like plodding up a steep hill in the driving rain and mud wearing oversized rubber boots that are full of water. So, we need to acknowledge that troubled projects do happen and there are steps we can take and tradeoffs we can make to help them along. Still, the vast majority of projects follow the plan well, provided it is well developed.

So, in Step 1, we finally begin our journey. Starting with Task 1a on our project schedule, we begin implementation. Beginning implementation is not at all like starting a football or basketball game.

In athletics, there is a lot of hype and buildup prior to the kickoff or tipoff. The larger the game, the greater the amount of hype and buildup. The Super Bowl is an excellent example of increased hype. Projects are different. No matter how large or complex a project, there just aren't the marching bands and blimps. Beginning project implementation may best be described as "beginning something big with a silent whimper."

It is only natural for us to correlate bells and whistles with the amount of work we had to do to get there. After all, our society correlates the two. The retirement party is an excellent example of this societal correlation between work (or money invested) and hype. The employer rewards the employee for working for 35 years by sending the faithful worker off on a cruise or by presenting the employee with a gold watch. So, it's natural for us to expect that hype will follow the preparatory work once the kickoff is announced. But in project management it just doesn't happen!

It is important for project managers to be prepared for emotional letdowns as a project begins. "Why do I feel so depressed? This is what we've been planning for and invested so much work in to this point. Why do I feel drained?" It's only natural. We have been wired to expect some sort of buildup, and it doesn't come with project implementation. What is the result? We experience a letdown. It happens to the most experienced and successful project managers. Once realized, however, we can understand and prepare for our emotional letdowns, deal with them more positively, and begin projects. Anticipating this potential let-down, we can plan some preventive measures—such as sponsoring a hype-package or kickoff mini-celebration.

In implementation, things can become jumbled, fast moving, and confusing. It needn't be that way. It is common, though, when the project manager and project management team move from the arena of planning to that of doing. Planning seems to involve patience. Implementation, on the other hand, doesn't involve any patience—it is demanding. The pace—at least the perceived pace—quickens. This is often met with increasing levels of anxiety. Because of this, it is easy to get caught up in all the details, the "have-to-do's," and miss the critical aspects of project implementation. The successful project manager needs to have these critical aspects indelibly stenciled into his or her forehead. These critical factors simplify the rush of details that accompany project implementation and help keep you focused on what is really important.

What are the critical factors for successful project implementation? There are four of them—schedule, communication, resource coordination, and budget.

Schedule: What did you spend most of your time accomplishing in the planning phase? Wasn't it to develop a well-reviewed, communicated, and tested map of the implementation journey? The project chart or schedule is the driver of project implementation. Like a detailed map, it provides the step-by-step, stop-by-stop, daily mileage, route-by-route description of the implementation. This is the critical pulse of the project. Like a secret code for deploying nuclear arms, the project schedule is never far from a successful project manager. It is reviewed regularly. It is posted in the project team's brain center. It is the first item of business thrown out on the table in the status meetings. It is the map to the treasure. When everything around seems confusing and too detailed, the successful project manager can never loose sight of the map. This is always the first consideration.

Why is the schedule the first consideration? Why isn't it the budget? After all, it can be argued, upper management is truly only interested in saving money. "Don't overrun the budget!" In reality, money is not a finite commodity. We too often treat it like it is, but it isn't. If something unexpected happens, we sometimes feel like we can always spend a little more money to fix it and get it done. Time, on the other hand, definitely is a finite commodity. You cannot create time. For this reason, the successful project manager knows that schedule is the most critical consideration. Time is not elastic—schedule is the number one priority!

Project: Installation of Anodic Ventilation System

Tasks	Duration	M	T	W	T	F	M	T	W	T	F	M	T	W	T	F	M	T	W	T	F	M	T	W	T	F	M	T	W
1. Begin Project																													
2. Quantify Evolution Rate																													
A. Conduct Monitoring	1 day																												
B. Get Results	2 weeks																												
C. Calculate Evolution	2 hours																												
3. Design Ventilation																													
A. Design Specifications	1 day																												
B. Determine Inlet	2 days																												
C. Select Fan	1 day																												
D. Design Electrical	2 days																												
E. Design Ducting	1 day																												
F. Design Discharge	1 day																												
G. Acquire Drawings	2 weeks																												
4. Install Ventilation System																													
A. Design Out for Bid	2 weeks																												
B. Select Contractor	1 day																												
C. Award Contract	3 days																												

D. Contractor to Install	90 days
5. Monitor Exposures	
A. Perform Monitoring	1 day
B. Calculate Exposures	2 hours
6. Project Completed.	

(TBD) = To be determine

There is a reality that successful project managers understand: As project manager, you cannot extend the length of time it takes to complete your project. Only a project sponsor can extend that time, and usually only with the blessings of upper management. It is too easy for us in the project trenches to just say, "Well, it's going to take a little longer than planned!" In reality, though, if our sponsorship tells us that an extension is not okay, it's not okay and we are left with what we sold to the sponsor(s) and upper management in the first place. This is a reality in project management.

Communication: There are a couple of simple rules about communication that are used in total quality and participative management. The first rule says that you want others to be able to throw away information that is not focused or is too detailed. On the other hand, you *never* want them to be in the deficit communication mode. Left in the deficit role, we leave the missing spaces and blanks for the imagination to fill. There is a fact about the human animal that needs to be noted here. In project management, no news is *not* good news! When we are missing needed information, our imagination naturally fills in the blanks with negatives. "Johnny hasn't called in as he was supposed to. Maybe he's had an accident and is unconscious lying in a ditch somewhere." "The boss hasn't told me he liked the report I wrote. I'll bet he hates it!" "Sara didn't call me back. She's probably angry at me." We seldom think positive thoughts when there is a gap in communication.

The second rule says that only the receiver, not the transmitter, can determine the right amount of communication. In projects, the project manager is the transmitter and everyone else is a receiver. Actually, this second rule dovetails nicely with the first. So, the combined rule for communication in successful project management is "communicate, communicate, communicate."

Obviously, there are two arenas for communication—internal and external. Internal communications are targeted at members of the project team or resources committed to the project. One of the most important forms of internal communication is the regular project status meeting. Depending on the length of the project, intervals are established and regular status meetings held at those intervals. Seldom is the interval greater than weekly. A working agenda works well in this format, where each member has a copy which becomes the weekly work list and reporting list for meeting participants. The project status meeting also brings the team up to speed on the entire project—the big picture—while focusing on individuals' parts of the big picture. This big picture/little picture perspective helps all those involved to understand the coordination and importance of each contribution to the project. It also serves to get questions answered and potential problems to the surface quickly and in a forum where team brainstorming can offer the best solutions.

External communications are also important to the project. External communications include external resources, sponsors, bosses, regulatory agencies, and important support functions such as purchasing, receiving, accounts payable, capital management, etc. Not only is regular and thorough communication important to external contacts, the form of the communication can also be critical. Each group may have preferred communication means or may be physically removed so overall communication becomes more complex. The successful project manager uses many forms of communication and never assumes that one form or channel of communication is ever enough. They use electronic means, face-to-face, telephone calls and messages, status memos, newsletters (in wide distribution projects), etc., to accomplish this critical need of external communications.

Resource Coordination: Resource coordination is something that project managers should be skilled at. Jobs in safety, health, and the environment are defined by being responsible for resource coordination without having authority over its successful accomplishment. This is a hallmark of our professions. In reality, however, we are seldom skilled at coordinating things outside our sphere of influence, which can become frustrating and emotionally draining. Many safety professionals just pretend this coordination deficit doesn't exist and choose to ignore it. Doing that can be very dangerous.

But the challenge of resource coordination is all about having responsibility without authority. Looking at the range of options we have available for coordination, we could hope it happens without any effort, beg and plead, or communicate and form commitment agreements. Forming commitment agreements is a negotiation skill. But once the agreements are achieved, coordination becomes a function of communication.

Budget: In assigning a leader to a project, upper management asks three things. First, "Know what we want accomplished." In other words, "Do the project and have it be successful on our terms." Second, "Get the project done on time." This is the number one consideration. And third, "Don't waste the organization's resources." In other words, management asks that the project be done within the allotted budget or as close to it as possible. Obviously, if these are the three things that authorizing management wants from us, like schedule, budget requires our undivided attention.

There are limits as to how much money we can spend. The first limit is the amount of the approved budget. This first limit cannot be a "soft" limit. A successful project manager must be committed to it as a "hard" limit. A great deal of his or her reputation depends on this limit being honored. The second limit is usually a 10 percent overrun. This is a "one trip back" cost. But, the project manager must realize that there are costs for the one trip back. It certainly does not come free. These costs include delayed costs that come back as baggage near the end of the project, following the completion of the project, and in subsequent projects. Comments like, "How much is it really going to cost?" or "Well, last time..." are verbalizations of these costs.

STEP 2: MONITOR AND MEASURE PROGRESS OF THE PROJECT

Step 2 is a two-fold one—monitoring and measuring the progress of the project. These activities are not the same. Monitoring is keeping track of critical elements. Measurement—what I like to call scorekeeping—is the visual representation of major aspects we monitor.

Let's draw an analogy from football. There are many elements of the game that are monitored. These include elapsed time; first downs; third down conversions; total rushing and passing yards; number of passes attempted, completed, and intercepted; number of sacks; and the number of penalties and yards assessed. Additional monitored activities and performances include individual tackles, team statistics by quarter and half, average yards per carry, average yards per reception, points scored, success rate in the red zone, number of punts and average yardage per punt, average beginning field position, number of field goal attempts and completion's, etc. Not all of the monitored elements show up on the scoreboard (i.e., receive real-time measurement). Usually the scoreboard displays only the score, which down it is, and how many yards to go for a first down, which quarter being played, and the time remaining in that quarter. These items are visually displayed because they are critical real-time indicators of the game and of the success of the teams who are playing. You can see from this example how measurement is both informational and motivational.

Of the four critical considerations for project implementation, only two can be monitored and measured—schedule and budget. Communication can only be monitored by the complaints or communication-caused problems that occur. And while resource coordination is a special function of the schedule, it is difficult to measure. But there are many other factors that are fingerprints of a successful project that can be monitored and may also need to be measured.

A note needs to be made concerning a lesson taught by Chuck Coonradt in his book, *The Game of Work*—monitor and measure results not activities. Using an example from sports, if you monitor the number of passes thrown by quarterbacks, this is an activity, a resource that must be activated in order to get the desired result. It bears, however, only a loose relationship to the results. What are the desired results? Of course, we want someone on the offense to catch the ball—we want the pass to be completed. But if we only monitor completions, it only tells us part of the story. So we measure the result as a function of the activity, what Coonradt calls the results to resources ratio. We measure completions per number of passes thrown. Likewise, if we measured copies made in a copy room of a company, this is only an activity. It serves as a resource to the desired result because you couldn't get the result without making copies, but what is the desired result? We want to make good, clean, perfect copies, not garbage. So we could monitor good, clean copies per total number of copies made as a performance indicator of copy room output. Projects are no different. We must monitor results and, if possible, marry them with the available resource that produces the desired result.

List of Project Results That Can Be Monitored

- Spent budget against total budget

- Spent budget against projected budget at this point in project

- Spent budget for major items against projected budget

- Ratio of tasks completed on time against total projects to date

- Days successfully into project against the plan or project schedule

- Problems avoided against those anticipated

- Time lost per unexpected problem

- Opportunities taken advantage of against those identified

- Days gained per opportunity

- Days invested in permitting against allotted days

- Cumulative downtime against projected downtime to date

- On-time delivery of tasks from resources against total resource tasks

---

Note that the provided list is for monitored results. This is important to note because we naturally fall prey to the connection that if we take the time to monitor it, then it stands to reason that we should measure it. That is, we need to put it up on the wall in some sort of visual display format. This correlation doesn't necessarily hold true. Monitoring the results against the available resources or activities is an indicator of whether your project is in or out of control. It is a tool a successful project manager can use to determine where he or she needs to invest a little more time before the project really gets off-track. Monitoring is like making sure the lug nuts on your car's wheels are tight. Monitored results are management tools.

Measurement or scorekeeping, on the other hand, is informational and motivational. The purpose of measurement is different than that of monitoring. If we measure everything we monitor, we invite everyone who views the scorekeeping to assist in managing the project. This is crazy and an invitation to chaos. However, if we don't measure the correct things, the important information that needs to be conveyed isn't, and no one becomes excited or motivated. Also, if critical information that needs to be measured is missed, key people to the project tend to become very anxious. Anxiety in key people, like sponsors, is not a positive influence on a project's stability and progress.

What are key informational and motivational results that should be measured? Here is a short list.

List of Project Results That Should Be Measured

- Spent budget against projected budget at this point in project

- Ratio of tasks completed on time against total projects to date

- Days successfully into project against the plan or project schedule

- Cumulative downtime against projected down time to date

What kind of measurement is best for this project? Should it be simple or complex? Is this a call for a graphics program or a piece of scratch paper? Should the presentation be three-dimensional and multicolored, or hand-written and drawn? What is best for project measurement?

The best advice is to follow the "six-year-old test." If your measurement is too complex for a six year old to immediately tell you if you are winning or not, it's too complex. After all, a six-year old can tell which football team is winning by looking at the scoreboard. Likewise, the less paper that is required, the less there is to get lost and the less work for you. After all, measurement is only a small part of your job as a project manager. It is a form of communication; it is certainly not your whole job. Keeping measurement simple and short is always the best answer.

If your efforts are successful in not exceeding the projected or allotted resources, pie graphs, as a function of project time, are probably the easiest to decipher. If the total pie represents the projected or allotted resource and dividing the pie shows a fraction used or spent, it is easy to derive whether or not you are successfully managing your project. Simple above-the-line or below-the-line bar graphs can be confusing if you don't know whether above or below is the desired outcome. Sometimes simple numbers can also be very easy to use. But whatever display method serves your purpose best, be consistent throughout your measurement. Consistency avoids confusion and questions.

STEP 3: EVALUATE AND MODIFY THE PROJECT PLAN AS NECESSARY

The settlers who ventured West during the mid-to-late 1900s had one critical tool. Without that all-important tool, none of them could have even begun their journey in the first place. That tool was a map. The explorers and earlier pioneers who went before developed that tool. It wasn't a perfect tool, but it was the best tool available. Along the way, as they discovered new information, found new passages, or had difficulties the map failed to warn them about, they improved the map they had. Over time and as the journey progressed, their map became full of notes, new discoveries penned in along the path they took, or question marks about information not found. Even the pioneers who went first knew that modification of the map was an expected part of any journey of discovery. It was part of their responsibility to improve the maps for others, who would, in turn, improve the maps again.

It is funny that we fully recognize this map development stage from our country's history to be true and reasonable, but reject such map modification in project management terms. Here our plan or map seems to become something deeply personal to us. After all, we spent all that time and energy getting the map or plan just right. Because of that investment, we find it nearly impossible to modify it in midstream or midjourney. But if we return to the analogy of the pioneers and the settlers, we should see that we, too, are merely making the best map we can at the time of the project inseption. Starting out across the plains and mountain ranges of the project's life, we discover first hand what we could only have imagined or guessed at in our planning effort. We should be able to make changes in that plan without thinking that our planning effort has been flawed.

Take as an example an experienced project manager who knew the critical importance of planning to the success of his project. He had done his planning well and developed an extensive project plan. It was so extensive that when he showed it to others who were key to the project, they asked to see only a portion of it because it was just too much in its entirety. It wasn't too far into the project that a simple but time-delaying problem sprang up. The project manager's plan quickly dispensed of the problem and the project moved on, but a couple of days delayed. An opportunity to make up time would occur, he assumed, in one of the upcoming tasks. But then another problem surfaced and what was an opportunity task suddenly became a problem task. Now the project manager was a week behind and 6 percent over budget at nearly 30 percent into the project. Undaunted by these setbacks, he pressed on.

At this point, the project manager began to look for tasks ahead in the schedule where time could be made up, becoming entirely focused on making up the lost ground. He began to pressure the assigned human resources, trying to find ways to shorten their task time. These people started to become a little annoyed with him. He had become so focused on making up the ground that he had forgotten to manage and communicate some of the elements of his plan. Consequently, he lost a few more days on the schedule and began to alienate some key people. His measurement faltered severely. At what should have been the halfway point in this project implementation, he was at only 43 percent. His budget was 9 percent over. Undaunted once again, he stayed the course.

The rest of the journey really isn't important for our example. The final result was that he ended up more than a month late and 17 percent over budget. He also caused the facility to miss some critical shipments to customers because of some lengthy and unscheduled downtime. Many of the key resource people on the project vowed they would never work with him again, and upper management wasn't too thrilled with his performance, either. In the post-mortem on the project, it was pointed out that on Day 12 of the project schedule, he was given a plan modification opportunity that would have turned everything around. It was discovered that if he would have modified the plan on day 12 by moving a couple of task sequences to parallel each other rather than be sequential, he could have easily completed the project a month earlier than projected and would have had time and money available for the unexpected problems that occurred. What was most shocking, however, was that the project manager saw this opportunity on Day 10 and chose not to utilize it. He wasn't in trouble on Day 10, but when he was finally in trouble a short time later, it was to late to go back. "Besides," he said, "the schedule was so good that I just couldn't bring myself to mess it up so early in the running."

His mistakes are just too human. We spend so much effort creating and perfecting something that we can't bring ourselves to change it, even when confronted with the possibility of disaster if we do not. A successful project manager must transcend this aspect of human nature.

He or she must not place the project plan on a pedestal, only to be followed and admired but not changed. The project schedule should be viewed as a best effort, a work in progress given our limited experience, lack of crystal ball vision of the future, or true knowledge of traps that await in project implementation. Because it is a best effort, it is seldom perfect and capable of withstanding all challenges. Because of this, we should be able and willing to modify it once we make that turn in the project road and get a closeup of reality.

It is also important to emphasize that as our knowledge improves with actual experience in the project, modification of the plan not only focuses contingency or corrective actions to avoid disaster, it also helps to surface previously unidentified opportunities. These are equally important for two reasons. First, we may need the ground we gain by banking these opportunities if unexpected and unplanned problems cause delays or cost unbudgeted excesses later down the road. Second, we should never miss a chance to be a hero. There just aren't that many heroic opportunities that we can afford to pass by due to our inattention. A project plan must remain semi-fluid. If it becomes cured in concrete, we lose.

It is an obvious point that the monitored comparison of results to resources can be an important source of information for evaluating the project plan. Monitored results to resources show us important trends in our project that point the successful project manager to look harder and focus his or her efforts ahead of the coming storm. This can be a significant leg-up to the observant project manager.

STEP 4: FINISH THE PROJECT

Yogi Berra stated, "It ain't over 'til it's over." And that applies to project implementation. There are two faces to this simple, funny statement. First, projects have a tremendous tendency to take on lives of their own; that is, they have a tendancy to never come to completion. Appendages spring up, almost by magic, like spontaneous generation from within the bowels of the project. "Well, while you're doing that, why don't you do this, too?" "Gee, half-way through we realized that if we added this part to the project, we could get more than we expected." Shazzammm! A new sticky or series of task stickies are attached to the schedule and the project continues on...and on...and on...ad nauseam. With all these new appendages, the project will never get done!

Second, when do we really *know* when done means done? We need to look back to the first step we transversed on our project management journey, dig out the original project statement, and revisit what we wanted to accomplish in the first place. If we wanted to install a ventilation system, when the final sign-off is completed, the project is complete. The project statement, conceived at the origin of the project, documents the finish line for the project. The objectives and constraints only tell you if what you accomplished was successful, not whether or not the project has been completed.

Even once the project implementation is complete, however, the project management process is not over. There are two important responsibilities ahead—communication and celebration. First, just because a project has been signed off on and deemed to be completely implemented, key people to the project and everyone impacted by it need to know that it has been successfully accomplished. This is both a signal for a return to normalcy and a statement of successful completion. It is also a time to emphasize the project's significant accomplishments with key sponsors and your boss. No time will be better than at completion to emphasize what you've accomplished and the status of the key measurements.

Second, project completion is also a time for celebration. Can you imagine an athletic contest that, once over, the combatants and interested spectators simply walked away without celebration? Of course you can't. Having been emotionally focused throughout the game, the winners and losers all have some sort of emotional response to it. If your team wins, you celebrate. It's automatic. Yet, when we are emotionally, mentally, and physically tied to a project, matching wits, planning resources against constraints, and battling against unknown problems and enemies, should we just sigh and walk away when it is completed? "Well, that's over." No! We deserve better! We deserve to celebrate with everyone who was involved in the project.

Celebration is not an immoral or excessive act; it is a release, a deserved fan fair or burst of fireworks. It is also a time for reflection and recognition of accomplishment. The level of celebration must be in proportion to the size and complexity of the project. If the project is to assemble a swing set in your backyard, a two-week trip to Europe to celebrate seems a little excessive. Big projects deserve big celebrations. But even little projects deserve celebrations, too. No project is too small that a celebration is not warranted.

STEP 5: DETERMINE THE LESSONS LEARNED

We tend to lose much of our memory power the longer we live. It has a lot to do with the aging process—the older we get, the less functional our memory mechanisms seem to be. Why is this important in a discussion of lessons learned? There's a simple but important correlation. Projects don't get accomplished overnight. The more complex, in general, the longer they take. So the amount we can learn from a project depends almost entirely on the availability of information that was gathered throughout the project management process. If we rely solely on our memory to retain this information, we will forget a lot of important lessons.

A colleague of mine has been managing projects for many years. He is also a proponent of the Japanese concept of *Kaizen*, or what we call continuous improvement. The lessons-learned step of the process is particularly valuable to him. He recognizes the critical tie of lessons learned to the act of capturing "lessons" along the project management path. He has a system to help him accomplish this. It isn't complex; it only requires discipline. Every time the project throws him a curve ball or offers up a fat pitch, he writes himself a dated note and puts it into his "Lessons Learned" envelope. I've seen him write himself two or three notes a day on some of the more challenging projects. When the project is finally signed off on and he moves to the lessons learned step, he dumps that envelope out on the table and starts sorting through it.

The important thing about his method of capturing lessons is that seldom do any lessons slip through the cracks and become lost due to the limitations of memory. Because of this simple system, the project manager can take maximum advantage of the lessons learned step, Step 5, of project management.

This example is a good overview of the six parts required in this step—capturing, compiling, dividing, analyzing, brainstorming, and documenting. The first part, *capturing*, is critical. A successful project manager knows that excellence in project management is a learning process. Experiences that occur during project management are excellent sources of information for further learning. There are many successful methods to capture this information during the management of the project. All of these methods require discipline to be effective. The example used above mentions notes thrown into an envelope. Other methods include a "discovery list," where a clipboard and pad of paper are placed in the project's brain center for listing unexpected occurrences and discoveries. Stickies can also be used to record information and to place a recommendation on the "trouble wall." Notes can also be made in a daily planner. Each of these methods has its strong and weak points. Other than discipline, the trick is to match the best method to your personal habits and daily routines. Even the best method, if it deviates too greatly from what is common practice for you, will be far more of a burden than a benefit. Select a convenient method that can be slipped into your routine activities. The less waves the system or method makes to your routine, the greater the quality of the information it can capture and provide for you later.

The second part, *compiling*, begins when Step 5 begins. Compiling is a data dump, one in which all the information is grouped so it can be more useful. For example, a group of twenty lesson areas is far more valuable than a pile of one thousand unsorted pieces of information. Individually, there is too much clutter and too much information. One could spend a lifetime looking through these individual pieces of information with seemingly no relationship to each other. The trick is to get all of the collected information into a few general areas so that each can be dealt with more effectively. This is what compiling is all about.

Common categories or areas that information can be compiled into include communication, resource scheduling/deployment, sponsor dealings/communication, monitoring and measurement, scheduling, people issues, safety/environmental planning, presentations and approvals, project concepts, budget issues, general lessons, etc. Depending on the area of expertise of the project involved, other categories become appropriate, such as permitting and public relations issues for environmental projects. The best practice is to not pre-limit the number of categories. As the compiling process continues, similarities will become more easily seen. Previously separated categories can later be combined.

The third part, *dividing,* focuses on a simple lesson about time. The lesson goes like this: If you had infinite time, you could do infinite tasks. Since you do not have infinite time, you can not achieve infinite tasks. End of lesson. Dividing involves categorizing compiled project information, then separating those categories into "big" and "little" issues. If you can't decide whether some items are big or little issues, create a middle pile. Keep working on the middle pile until only two remain. Staple the "little issue" pile together and when you get that elusive infinite time, you can deal with those. For now, the "big issue" pile is of greater importance. Continue dividing all categories until you have only big issues left to deal with.

After dividing up the number of information pieces, you should end up with about a 1 to 4 ratio of categories, big to little. If your categories are opposite, 4 to 1 big to little, you need to recalibrate and do it again. This division allows the successful project manager to focus his or her efforts on the information that will net the most learning and the most improvement. The "big issue" piles now can become the focal point of the project manager's attention.

The fourth step, *analyzing,* begins with a lessons-learned table or spreadsheet. Each big issue is placed in text fashion as bullets in the table. Each issue is then analyzed to find the most probable cause (singular), as shown in the following example.

Lessons-Learned Table

Information Captured	Most Probable Cause	
3. Communications:		
At first, team couldn't communicate effectively	New team formation made up of virtual strangers	
Communication quickly broke down in upper management presentation	Different languages: I used technical terms and they wanted economic	
Boss couldn't understand project schedule graph	Boss is a generalist and not technically trained	
E-mail seemed to not be an effective means	Not everyone has E-mail and they don't access daily	

When identified information has more than one base cause, a second level of dividing is in order. If one cause seems to be 80 percent of the reason and the other cause 20 percent, select the 80 percent cause for your table. If one cause is 60 percent and the other is 40 percent, however, you had better write both down in your table. The value of this step is to further refine the issues you need to learn from. In order to achieve this, the major causes of your big issues need to be included. This further focuses your lessons-learned efforts so that you can be more successful in improvement of the project management process.

Don't expect to solve all the problems in one lesson. It just can't happen that quickly. Successful analysis is a part of the continuous improvement process. It can only happen over time. The major issues of a project should, however, be resolved through the lessons learned in this step. Hopefully, those will not reappear in future projects. Some lesser issues and lesser causes will appear again, of course, in later projects. They will become another lesson learned. Once they advance to the big issue piles of that other project, or once they are considered a repeated obstacle, they must be dealt with and resolved as a continuation of the lessons-learned process.

The fifth step, *brainstorming,* is a step that finds the best solution for resolving the most probable cause. One important consideration needs to be pointed out here—that the best solution needs to be under your team's control or influence. This includes the control or influence of the project sponsor. This point is important because if you make a "blue sky" solution like "create a need for world peace," you don't have a realistic chance of resolving the issue at hand. The resolution of the probable cause must be reasonably obtainable and practical. Brainstorming returns us to our lessons-learned table example.

Lessons Learned Table

Information Captured	Most Probable Cause	Best Solution
3. Communications:		
At first, team couldn't communicate effectively	New team formation made up of virtual strangers	Team building training prior to project start-up
Communication quickly broke down in upper management presentation	Different languages: I used technical terms and they wanted economic ones	I will learn more economics and use them in my project presentations
Boss couldn't understand project schedule graph	Boss is a generalist and not technically trained	Begin teaching boss by routing articles to him
E-mail seemed to not be an effective means	Not everyone has E-mail and they don't access daily	Follow-up all e-mails with telephone calls

The last part, *documentation,* transfers the best solutions into a format that can be tracked and followed to completion. Obviously, the table can be easily expanded to include "Assigned To," "Due By," "Follow-Up," and "Completed" columns. Often times, this is the best method of keeping all the information in one place and of not wasting efforts copying information that has already been captured in written form.

STEP 6: PROJECT CLOSE OUT AND DOCUMENTATION

This step is the "putting things away, turning out the lights and closing the door" step. With the project completed, everything needs to be put in order and finalized. Step 6 has two purposes. It is the official close to the project and it documents the details of project management into one source.

The official close of a project revisits everything that was accomplished—each task, each step—to assure that everything was indeed completed. If anything was missed, it must be brought to closure before the project can be closed out. Was all documentation completed? Were all tasks accomplished? Were all project steps and project management phases completed? Were the lessons learned put into an action format so that they could be analyzed? Was everyone impacted by, dependent upon, responsible for, or sponsoring the project notified of the project completion and its successes? When all steps have been taken, all tasks accomplished, and all communication completed, only then can the project be closed out.

The documentation of project management includes detailing what was done, when, and how. It also includes identification of those involved. Important project documents must be included, such as purchase orders for resources or equipment, delivery tickets, written communications, completed to-do lists, etc. This final documentation should be treated like a time capsule. It should include every important detail for anyone who wants or needs the information in the future. This documentation should not be scattered thinly throughout the organization—in different files, in different departments, and in different people's desks. It needs to be gathered in one place, such as in an engineering project file or in an equipment or process file to be maintained by mechanical integrity programs.

A colleague probably said it best when he summarized what project documentation is all about: "I might get hit by a Mack truck tomorrow, so it is my responsibility to document everything in one place so that someone else can simply pick up my file and continue on, never losing a step." This is perhaps a rather graphic interpretation, but it keenly points at what documentation is all about.

SUMMARY

Phase III: Project Implementation

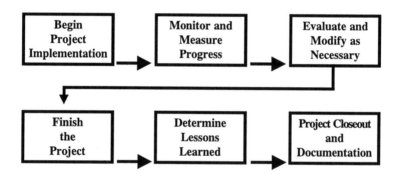

Phase III of project management is where most ill fated projects failed. They may have defined what they want to get done and just go do it, but until Phase III, all of this is only theoretical. The steps in both Phase I and Phase II are critical to making Phase III successful. So, the entirety of most traditional projects is contained in this one simple and moderately short chapter, although it may seem very short and stark. But reality is very stark, isn't it?

The opening volley began in this phase. In Phase III, we actually began moving dirt, putting up scaffolding, setting forms, etc. This phase began the "action" part of the project, which is separated from the preparatory, "thinking" parts of it. In project implementation, we closely watch the schedule or plan, the communication, the resource coordination and the budget. As the implementation continues, we begin to monitor our progress. We closely monitor and measure the schedule and the budget restrictions. But encapsulated in this step is also an active monitoring of several key performance indicators or results—including budget breakdowns, time and schedules, problems and opportunities, downtimes, and on-time issues. These indicators provide information on how to invest our limited and valuable time and efforts. From this monitoring, we constantly reevaluate and modify our plan, as necessary. Finally, we finish the project. We know when we finish a project because we see that we have accomplished what our project statement said we would. Then we can celebrate the victory. In what seems to be a short flurry of activity, the project is begun and is completed.

Moving back into a detail mode, we take a hard look at all of the collected pieces of information about problems, communication, questions, and opportunities that are collected throughout the project management process and then carry out a six-part approach to ultimately come up with prevention plans. These results will help us to continually improve our project management abilities and our process in the future. Then, at last, we must double-check everything, complete our project communications, fully document the project, put it all together, and close it out.

Phase III of project management begins with action and ends in thought, completing the cycle of the first two phases, which are all about thought. But it remains the "thinking" aspects of all three phases that either makes project management successful, or drives it into being an overwhelming challenge. Successful project management is all about thought. The doing it comes easy, if the mechanisms for thorough thought are in place and practiced before the action begins.

6

PROJECT MANAGEMENT TOOLS

Toolmaking is one of the key elements that anthropologists say separates us from other beasts. We humans have a long history of making tools. What is the purpose? Tools make the task or job easier. Tools, of course, constitute a continuum, a dynamic process of improvement.

Consider early man's construction of an animal skin that could carry objects. It was an effective tool for carrying many small items or gathering food. Tool building is a human dynamic. Once an easier way to do it was found, the tool was improved. If the animal skin were elongated, it could be slung over the shoulder. More could be carried, including heavier objects. The animal skin pack became even more refined and improved to carry even heavier objects. The pack was further modified and placed on a frame of wood to carry objects, which became another tool, and it was dragged by one or more people.

Animals became domesticated and both of these tools were put together to carry even more. Then the wheel was invented and the packs took on the form of a cart. The cart went through many centuries of improvements in wheel construction, cart design, wheel and axle lubrication, etc. The cart became continually modified and specialized to meet specific needs from carrying people, to racing, to carrying large burdens, to putting houses on wheels.

Carts evolved into barges and ships that carried objects and people across large expanses of water. Wind power was harnessed. Specialized boats moved up and down rivers, in shallow and deep water.

Eventually, they became large enough to conquer the forces of the ocean.

Then rubber was invented. Ball bearings improved the cart further. The steam engine was invented and railroads became the improved land-cart. The internal combustion engine came and man discovered the automobile. Automobiles became trucks. Carts moved into the sky as airplanes, no longer needing roads. Newer and newer engines were discovered. Space became the specialized cart's frontier for hauling things and people.

Toolmaking is a dynamic and continually improving concept. Here are some facts we must keep in mind when looking at project management tools. Fact 1: Project management tools are constantly improving, especially with the constant and rapid improvement in computers and software. Fact 2: This is not a "one size fits all world." That is, no one tool for project management can fit every need. Some project managers need a simple tool. Others want or need a very complex, computerized tool. Some want their tool to be simple. Others want to collect every possible detail and bit of information. No one tool for project management will fit all our needs and desires. Too often we forget this and only look at the most advanced tools—often computerized tools. Even today, computerized tools are not the tool-of-choice of more than 75 percent of the project management applications. This is an important starting point for us in our search for project management tools.

PROJECT MANAGEMENT TOOL OPTIONS

When one seeks out tools for use in project management, there are two basic tool options: You can use computerized or paper-based (manual) project management tools. Both options have advantages and drawbacks. Which option you choose depends on the complexity of your projects and how much you like to be tied to a computer. As an example, many use computers to plan their day, schedule their appointments, keep their telephone and address information, and perform other day-to-day efficiency matters. Others feel that it is too restrictive to be tied to a computer so they use a day planner or some other form of written information tracking system. Both options meet that person's particular likes and needs.

We tend to get caught up in fads. In fads, we tend to devalue our needs and focus only on the fad. Unfortunately, this is the way we often approach computerization. A new software package comes out and because it is on a computer, we assume it has to be better. So, in response to our fad thinking, we buy the software, load it on our computer and attempt to merge the software with our routines, habits, and daily constraints. Sometimes we are successful and the software does fit our needs. In that case, we keep using those software packages and tend to update them when they advance. More often, however, we find that forced-use of the software becomes more of an efficiency drain than a benefit. The dependence on the computer just doesn't merge with our cadence, mobility, or daily routines. So, we abandon the computerized approach and return to the manual, paper-based method. Fad chasing produces predictable results.

There's another way to split the available project management tool options. You can either choose to pay for a project management tool or you can choose to use a free one. Many think, why pay for something you can get for free? They haven't always found that paying for something necessarily makes it better or more convenient.

It is important to note that no commercially available manual or computerized project management tool can alone complete all the necessary steps for successful project management. The manual methods you buy often do better, but they, too, are incomplete. The computerized tools seem to want to "shorthand" the process. Because of these shortcomings, if you choose to use commercial tools, it's important to insert the tools into the project management process rather than using them as *the* process.

COMPUTERIZED PROJECT MANAGEMENT TOOLS

There are a few project management software options. In reality, all are very similar, although each has its specific "bells and whistles" that manufacturers use to differentiate it from the others. As with most other software, the established standard is a program from Microsoft called Project. We'll use Project as an example of available software packages in our discussion.

Advantages: There are distinctive advantages to using software for project management. First, the programs allow the project manager to automatically tie key project management steps together. In fact, the format of the program requires it. Second, because everything is tied together, the project manager usually only has to enter the information once. The program shuffles the information around into different formats. Third, this software allows information to be displayed in different modes that can help to visually manage or troubleshoot schedules, tasks, or resource allocations. For example, the program can display schedule information in *both* vertical task breakdowns and horizontal process flows. Fourth, this software automatically checks for mistakes such as whether a particular resource has been over-scheduled. Fifth, it will usually determine a critical sequence and highlight it for easy identification. The responsibility remains the project manager's, however, to correctly identify sequences so that the software can do this. Providing different visual displays allows the user to see the critical sequence and determine key dependent tasks that need extra management efforts. Sixth, revising the plan is very simple—the project manager just changes a variable and everything shifts. This can be particularly helpful in the early stages of project planning when task duration is soft, unknown, or, at best, a guess. And seventh, most software packages will automatically tie the schedule to a calendar format. Having tasks displayed on a calendar can make schedules more friendly and clear. These are some of the significant advantages that project management software has for project managers.

Disadvantages: There are downsides to project management software as well. First, the project manager is locked to the computer. At the job site, in planning meetings, etc., he or she is left with the paper image of the computerized record. Any modification or detailed information requires sitting down in front of the computer screen and pecking it in. Field modifications or on-site urgent changes require the project manager to fly by the seat of his or her pants because the hard copy information is restrictive and may not be complete. Second, since modification can be too convenient, electronic projects often can have several "editions" or "revisions" on the table at the same time. Not knowing which printout is the official, blessed, absolutely final, or current plan can cause tremendous confusion. Third, the user is bound by the software programming. In many ways, the user may want different displays or information tied in a certain way that is not available in the software package or that he or she does not know how to produce because of limited knowledge of the software's capabilities.

Fourth, most software does not share information with other similar applications. For example, one project manager could be using project management software while a fellow engineer is using the exact same software package to manage his or her project. Both of them could be depending on using the same limited resource on the same day and neither would know it, even if they were networked together. This is an important negative because too often we think that computerized methods are next to perfect. We mistakenly believe that they will take care of everything when, in fact, they won't. But, because of our mistaken belief, we slack-off on some of the other critical elements of project management, assuming that it is a "done deal." So, we don't check things out as well as we should and we don't communicate as thoroughly as we need to. If we don't send the plan through after the thorough review and critique it needs, it can emerge flawed, as can the plan of the fellow engineer. This spells double trouble to an organization. Now, instead of having a single fatal error, it has two existing errors on parallel paths. This is a significant problem in organizations that manage a large number of projects at a time.

Fifth, the software locks the project manager into hardware needs or restrictions. For instance, buying a $450 software package may require the user to spend an additional $750 upgrading the computer it's running on, or $30,000 upgrading the department's computer system or PCs, or require the purchase of specialized printers, such as color printers or printers that accommodate a variety of paper sizes. These upgrades and purchases are not cheap. In other words, it is easy to justify a $450 purchase, but that may tie the user into a much more extensive purchase of software and hardware.

Sixth, software exists in a different time warp. Just when the user gets the latest version and learns how to use all it's "bells and whistles," the software manufacturer upgrades it and he or she is back to spending money, upgrading hardware, and learning the new capabilities all over again. This in itself can be a derailing negative for those who are too busy in the first place.

Seventh, when computerized project management tools become *the* tool, they can create a trap that results in incomplete planning. This is primarily a function of how easy it is to use computers to get smart looking documentation. It is easy to miss some of the critical steps in project management and think that just because it looks professional, the user must have done a thorough job of planning, communicating, etc. This can be a significant drawback to computerized tools for those who are forgetful or who are tempted to "just get on with it" before completing the necessary planning.

Eighth, computerized programs tend to "magic wand" project management. Since everything is programmed in, it is easy to use and some never really understand the important aspects of project management and why they are important. This can be a significant organizational trap where project management becomes so entrenched in a computerized system that the project management skills are lost or not improved. Skill degeneration and not having a continuously improving system are significant disadvantages. Whether a computerized tool is standardized in an organization or not, it is paramount that training on manual project management be a requirement and that some form of continuous improvement be included.

In any event, software packages provide very impressive documents. After all, continous improvement of software prompts the project manager to continue buying upgrades, and that's what software companies target on. For example, look at the following Gantt chart from Microsoft Project. As you will note, it looks very impressive.

Major project stages are displayed boldly. Critical sequence tasks are displayed in a visually different way to make them easily seen. Tasks are connected by arrows so you can easily see the flow of tasks. Assigned people are identified on the Gantt together with the effort level for all assigned. Task durations are shown in a separate column and easily determined by the length of the task marker. This, you will have to admit, is pretty slick.

But, as I stated earlier, don't get caught up in all the "bells and whistles." The format of the documents is great, but the advantages in total must outweigh the disadvantages. This dependence cannot be forgotten.

MANUAL OR PAPER-BASED PROJECT MANAGEMENT TOOLS

Advantages: Like computerized project management tools, manual methods have definite advantages and disadvantages. The first advantage of the manual tool is trustworthiness. We tend to trust best what we can tangibly get our hands on, carry around, and scribble on. Paper-based tools just seem more "trustworthy" because of this tangible nature. A second advantage is that manual tools are portable. The user is not locked to a computer station for updating or accessing information. All he or she needs is a file that can be carried to meetings, job sites, and boss's offices, or even across the country. A third advantage is that manual project management tools are convenient to modify or update. Depending on the specific tool used or on techniques for collecting and sorting information, they can be greatly advantageous to update.

A fourth advantage is that updating with a manual tool is always easily identified because the most current version is easy to pick out. For this reason, there is usually less confusion about what revision the team is working on or has a copy of. A fifth advantage comes from the fact that since our society is well adapted to paper systems, getting copies of information is always just a copy machine away. This is a major advantage. Because everything is written down and kept together in a paper system, it is hard to lose information. In a computerized

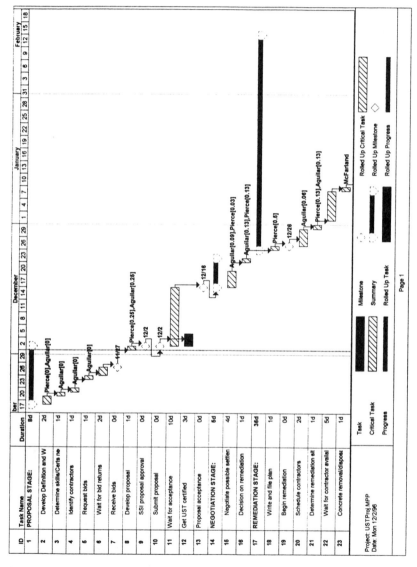

Microsoft Project Gantt Chart-Sheet 1

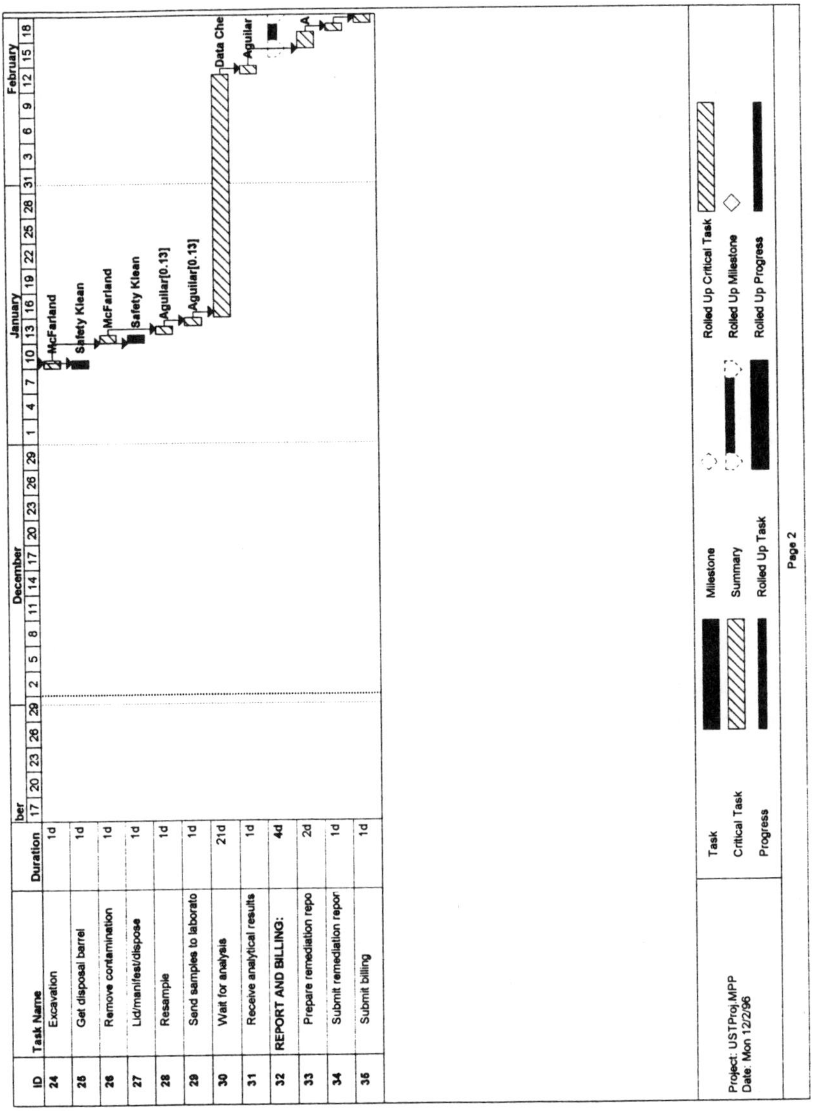

Microsoft Project Gantt Chart-Sheet 2

system it is too easy to lose. That delete key and overwriting just works too well. In paper systems, information may get junkie but it is always there. Tracing information back to its origins or timing is also much easier in a paper-based system.

A seventh advantage is that collecting important pieces of information is easier because of the written format of the plan and the all-togetherness of the project documentation. Having a lessons-learned sheet in the folder is a very convenient and effective means of capturing and collecting this important data. An eighth and final advantage of using a paper-based project management system is that most commercially available manual methods come with more aids and training than computerized programs. Because manual tools tend to require structure that is automatic in computerized tools, required training or process certifications are required before use. This can also be a disadvantage because of the additional costs of training, which can be significant. But, overall, the largest advantage is that there is less of a "magic wand" approach to project management with a manual tool. A manual system requires the manager to really be familiar with what he or she is doing, rather than just having tasks automatically created, formatted, and replaced by the computer.

Disadvantages: There are some real disadvantages to manual project management as well. Specific commercially available paper systems sold by a number of companies each have their good points and bad points. Depending on what system a project manager chooses, he or she is pretty much locked in to doing project management their way. Second, whereas updating is convenient, getting a clean copy of the current revision, especially those of revision number 20 or greater can be difficult because those revisions tend to be very messy. Making a clean copy of the 30th revision is time-consuming. This is the real advantage of the computerized systems over manual ones. Third, because everything is manually created, different views of information take extra time. It is logical to put items in a vertical task breakdown. Changing to a horizontal format from that requires extra effort. Fourth, the user has to manually tie together important data and information. This task is automatic using computerized software tools. Fifth, unless the user checks and double checks, he or she can overutilize some resources. This is especially true if the project is very large or very complex. Resource allocation tends to become hidden in busy projects that use manual methods.

The rule of thumb about whether a project manager should use a computerized or manual project management system isn't really that complex. If the projects being worked on tend to be very large or very complex, the advantages of the computerized tools may be of greater significance. If, however, the projects are smaller or more streamlined, it doesn't seem to make much sense to computerize them. It is a lot like killing a housefly with a cannon. The point is that everything has its place. The purpose of either tool is to standardize the process, regardless of whether that is being done by a computerized or manual tool, and to tap into a project management process that makes it easier for the project manager to control the project. After all, it's the formal, standardized process that makes project management successful, *not* the tool.

There are many commercially available project management tools. Perhaps the best known and respected is the project management technique marketed by Kepner-Tregoe, Inc. Rather than reviewing all the manual tools, we will take a look at the one they offer.

The Kepner-Tregoe system has a sequence of steps, like the ones noted in this book, but their system misses or omits many critical steps that they assume will be accomplished. Because project management is such a structured process, this can be a dangerous assumption. But steering away from this concern, let's focus on the paper-based tools this manual method provides.

Commercially available systems like Kepner-Tregoe provide forms for everything. This is good because a "packet" will force the project manager to jump through all the right hoops. For example, a form for project definition requires a project statement and identification of project objectives (noted as "At the end of project we will have:"). Kepner-Tregoe utilizes a tree-type vertical task breakdown structure and numbering system as shown on the next page.

Like the horizontal process mapping technique discussed in this book, this method provides a visual layout of the tasks, sequences, and dependences. This is a helpful tool but stickies can be even more convenient and easily shuffled around the paper when a step or task is forgotten or suddenly discovered.

Specialized vertical work breakdown structure sheets are also provided. In an effort to minimize the amount of coping information, the task list is placed on carbonless-copy pages, which allows the information in certain columns to be seen on multiple sheets in the pack. The first sheet in the Kepner-Tregoe system is devoted to identifying resource requirements for each listed task (knowledge/skills, facilities, equipment, materials, special resources, resource costs, and notes). The second sheet focuses on responsibility assignments. The third allows the project manager to diagram the sequence of deliverables. This is convenient for determining critical sequence but constitutes another mapping chore. The fourth sheet is for constructing a Gantt chart of the project (a third mapping exercise of the project).

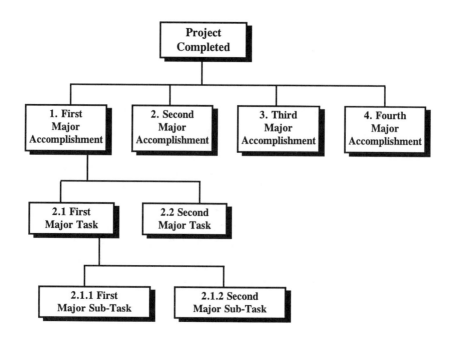

Other convenient worksheets provided in the Kepner-Tregoe packet include those devoted to potential problem analysis (planning phase) and checklists for close out and evaluation (implementation phase). But the heart of the Kepner-Tregoe project management system is their process and project work breakdown structure pack.

With any program you purchase and use, you buy a process. Often, due to the locked-nature of the process, you are locked into that approach and the included steps. Obviously, there are five distinct roads you can take. 1) You can buy a system, either manual or computerized, and live with what you get. 2) You can implement a detailed project management process that uses all your steps and phases and insert a computerized tool that automates the planning aspects. 3) You can implement a detailed project management process and insert the additional steps or worksheets into a purchase manual system. 4) You can implement a detailed project management process and use both a computerized tool (for large or complex jobs) and a manual tool with inserted steps and worksheets. Notice that the key, but unwritten, action word in these first four options is "buy." It is a money exchange where you purchase something and import it into or have it become your process. There is one last option. 5) You can implement a detailed project management tool that is complete and free.

A WORKSHEET APPROACH TO PROJECT MANAGEMENT

As stated earlier, project management is a *learned skill*. Too often, because of all the commercial options that are available, we tend to think that project management is only a "purchased process." This just isn't true! To believe this is to give away some of our personal power in the management process. By capitulating to this "purchased process" thinking, we accept the limitations of the particular process we purchase and use, perhaps giving away a better, less restrictive choice. However, if we choose not to purchase a project management process or technique, we take the first step toward acquiring personal power over the method or tool, and its connected restrictions. Once we come to the awareness that no matter what tool we choose to use, it will only be part of our personal project management process, we can see that project management truly is a "learned skill." The important connection of this discovery is, of course, that we don't have to purchase a tool at all.

Throughout the last three chapters, I've detailed a proven, effective process for successful project management. From those discussions, let's look at a worksheet approach utilizing this three-phase, eighteen-step process for project management.

Project Management Phase I: Concept and Approvals

Step 1: Identify Project Concept, Major Goals and Risks
Developing a Project Statement:

1. **Result:** What is the end result or accomplishment of the project? (*Be Specific, e.g.: Implement a program, build a building, install a piece of equipment.*)

2. **Budget:** How much will it cost *or* how much budget is allocated?

3. **Time:** When does the project have to be done?

4. **Project Statement:** Combine information from 1-3 above into a clearly worded statement.

[I:A]

---

5. **Value:** In what way(s) will this project provide documentable value to the organization?

6. **Risks:** What are the risks to the project and the organization? (List)

[I:B]

Project Management Phase I: Concept and Approvals

Step 2: Identify Project Objectives and Constraints

1. **Objectives:** Once completed, what will be the *measurable* benefits? (What must the project be able to do?)

2. **Constraints:** What limiting factors must also be successfully met?

   Time limitations:

   Resource limitations:

   Conflicts:

   Codes/Standards/Permits/etc.:

   Others:

[I:C]

Project Management Phase I: Concept and Approvals

Step 3: Obtain Preliminary Approval for the Project

   1. "Package" the information appropriately and effectively.

      What format will be used?

      What information is needed?

   2. Who needs this information and what lead-time is best?

      Person/Position   *By what time?*

[I:D]

3. What is the urgency of the project?

   Are approval discussions/meetings/presentations aligned with this urgency?

4. What questions can you anticipate and what information do you need to have prepared before time?

   Questions: *Needed Information:*

[I:E]

Project Management Phase I: Concept and Approvals

Step 4: Identify the Major Project Elements and Create a Project Map

1. Using small "stickies," identify all the major project elements, put them in order, and then number each. (Rule: No more than eight major elements!)

> **Begin the Project**

> **Complete the Project**

[I:F]

2. Identify all tasks on the vertical Project Work Breakdown Sheet and assign a realistic duration to each task.

3. In the space below, create either a vertical or horizontal project map showing task sequence, dependence, and duration. (**Helpful Hint:** To minimize repetition, use only task numbers from vertical work breakdown.)

| 1 | **Project**
Begins (No Duration)

Project Completion
(No Duration)

[I:G]

Project Work Breakdown Sheet

Phase/Task	Duration	Resources	Assignment

[I:H]

Project Management Phase I: Concept and Approvals

Step 5: Identify Project Resource Needs
Using the Project Work Breakdown Sheet, identify the appropriate resources for each task.

Project Management Phase I: Concept and Approvals

Step 6: Obtain the Go-Ahead Approval for the Project
1. Identify the essential outcomes for project success:

Budget:

Resources:

Time:

Sponsorship:

Contract:

[I:I]

2. Plan your approval-seeking meeting/presentation.

Who needs to be there?

What presentation/information conveying tools will you use?

When is the meeting/presentation?

What specific information do you need to provide?

What questions can you anticipate and what additional information do you need to have?

[I:J]

Project Management Phase II: Planning and Analysis

Step 1: Assign Project Jobs and Tasks

Using the Project Work Breakdown Sheet, assign specific responsibility to each task and oversight/management responsibility to each major project element. (**Helpful Hint:** Assign responsibilities to persons, not teams or departments.)

Project Management Phase II: Planning and Analysis

Step 2: Establish Critical Sequence of Tasks and Dependent Tasks

Using the project map completed for Phase I, Step 4, Number 3, add up all possible task sequences from project beginning to completion. Highlight the one sequence route that has the fewest days. This is the Critical Sequence.

Project Management Phase II: Planning and Analysis

Step 3: Develop and Chart Project Schedule

1. Fold the Project Chart Sheet at the left border and tape it to the right border of the Project Work Breakdown Sheet.
2. At the top of the Project Chart Sheet, record the appropriate calendar dates or days.
3. **Gantt Chart:** Beginning with Task 2A, record each task's duration vertically using line or block legend means.
4. Highlight the Critical Sequence of Tasks.

Project Chart Sheet

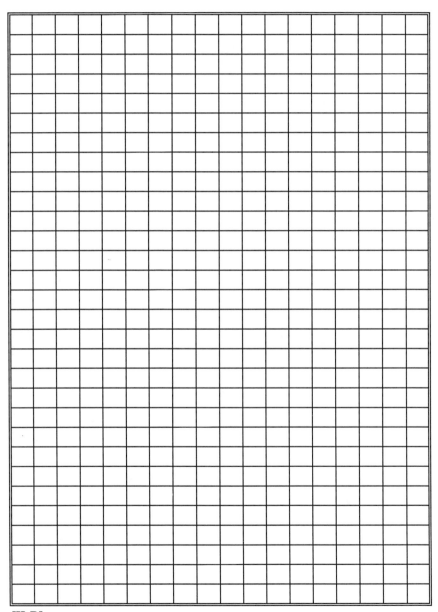

[II:B]

Project Management Phase II: Planning and Analysis

Step 4: Schedule Resource Deployment
Identify key resource people to be included in this step.

Helpful Hints for Successful Project Managers

1. Include key resource people in planning discussions.

2. Share a copy of the final project plan with key resource people.

3. Make sure pre-task communication is adequate for importance of task and schedule.

4. Include post-task communications for collecting lessons-learned information.

[II:C]

Project Management Phase II: Planning and Analysis

Step 5: Identify Potential Problems and Make Prevention Plans

1. Using the Problem Prevention Sheet, use the following criteria to identify potential problem tasks.

   - List tasks, critical or noncritical, that require the most resources or are the most complex.
   - List tasks that have the tightest assigned durations.
   - List tasks that are critical to more than one dependent task downstream.
   - List tasks that are accomplished by resources totally outside your control or influence.
   - List tasks that are assigned to resources who, in the past, have been less than dependable.
   - List tasks that are assigned to resources who are or are apparently over-booked or overworked.
   - List tasks that are led by members of management or the project management team who are less dependable, overly committed, or busy.

2. For each, determine what could cause the problem.
3. Identify a simple but specific prevention plan for each.
4. Stratify the potential problem task list by severity of outcome (high versus low).
5. Stratify the high severity potential problem tasks by probability of occurrence (high versus low).
6. Transfer preventive actions of high probability/high severity potential problem tasks to project plan.
7. Identify possible triggers that can be used early for prevention plan implementation.

[II:D]

Problem Prevention Sheet

List of Potential Problem Tasks   **Cause of Problem**   **Prevention Plan**

[II:E]

Project Management Phase II: Planning and Analysis

Step 6: Identify Potential Opportunities for Making Up Ground

1. Using the Opportunity Planning Sheet, use the following criteria to identify potential opportunity tasks.

   - List tasks, critical or noncritical, that require the least resources or are the least complex.
   - List tasks that have the most liberal assigned durations.
   - List tasks that can be done ahead of schedule.
   - List tasks that are accomplished by you or by resources who are totally under your control or influence.
   - List tasks that will get no attention or are really window dressing.
   - List tasks that are assigned to resources who have the reputation of getting work done early.
   - List tasks that are assigned to resources who are underbooked and underworked.
   - List tasks that are led by members of management or of the project management team who are always dependable or not busy.

2. Identify a simple but specific plan for taking advantage of each.
3. Stratify the potential opportunity task list by the amount of time each could make up (high versus low).
4. Stratify the high makeup potential opportunity tasks by probability of occurrence (high versus low).
5. Transfer opportunity actions of high probability/high makeup potential opportunity tasks to project plan.
6. Identify key potential problem tasks upstream that could trigger the need to focus on an opportunity task.

[II:F]

Opportunity Planning Sheet

List of Potential Opportunity Tasks   **Opportunity Actions**

[II:G]

Project Management Phase III: Project Implementation

Step 1: Begin Implementation

1. Identify the areas of special attention during project implementation.

   Schedule:

   Communication:

   Resource Coordination:

   Budget:

   Other:

2. What mechanism(s) will be used to capture lessons for learning?

[III:A]

Project Management Phase III: Project Implementation

Step 2: Monitor and Measure Progress of the Project

1. List results to resources ratios that will be monitored during the project.

Budget Items:

Schedule Items:

Problem Items:

Opportunity Items:

Interface Items:

Other Items:

[III:B]

2. List what will be measured and how.

Measured Ratio   **X/Y Axis**   **Display**

Where will these measures be visible?
How will key management/impacted people be apprised
of measures?

[III:C]

Project Management Phase III: Project Implementation

Step 3: Evaluate and Modify the Project Plan as Necessary
List the rules you will use for reviewing and modifying the project plan.

Who will make decisions on modifying the plan?

List plan modifications below.

[III:D]

Project Management Phase III: Project Implementation

Step 4: Finish the Project

1. List those who must be communicated with when the project is complete.

2. Detail your celebration plans.

[III:E]

Project Management Phase III: Project Implementation

Step 5: Determine Lessons Learned

1. **Capturing:** List all pieces of potential lessons learned information and list on an independent sheet.

2. **Compiling:** Group information into broad project categories.

3. **Dividing:** Separate the listed information under each broad project category into big issues and little issues. Put the major issues on the Lessons Learned Table.

4. **Analyzing:** Determine the probable cause (singular) for each big lesson.

5. **Brainstorming:** Identify the most likely preventive action.

6. **Documenting:** Transfer the information to your on-going planning schedule.

[III:F]

Lessons-Learned Table

Information Captured	Most Probable Cause	Planned Preventive Action

Project Management Phase III: Project Implementation

Step 6: Project Close Out and Documentation

1. Review the project information and be sure that everything is complete.

2. List all key people involved in the project.

3. Include applicable notes and after thoughts on the project.

[III:H]

A checklist approach to project management solves a number of mental and process problems for the project manager. It installs a project management process, of our own design, which meets our own needs. This formal standardization of our personal process is important. With its help, we're less likely to miss important steps throughout a complex process. It also allows us to impart what we learn back into the process. Points we need to remember or additions that meet our organization's needs can be simply added to the formal checklist. This is a continuous improvement process where we can further develop our project management skills.

SUMMARY

There are many tools we can use for project management. We can purchase both computerized and manual tools. Both have been developed with a lot of expertise and allow us to instantly capture all of this information into our process for project management. However, each tool comes with a certain amount of baggage that may limit its effectiveness for a specific project. Finding a tool that dovetails exactly is often the hardest element of a project. In purchasing a process for project management, we risk giving away "skill development" for a purchased, this-way-only, restrictive tool. Whether this is good or bad to an organization can only be answered on an individual basis. But by doing so, we out-source the learning portion of continual improvement and commit ourselves and our organizations to the restrictions of the tool and to the "learning" the tool manufacturer provides us.

We can also choose to use our own process—such as the checklist provided in this chapter or something like it. Recognizing that project management is a learned skill that must be continually improved, a checklist approach offers some definite advantages. It is less restrictive, it is more easily modified to meet our specific needs and limitations, and it allows us a convenient way of improving the skill in a formalized manner. These can be significant advantages to an organization.

7

PROJECT MANAGEMENT STANDARDIZATION IN AN ORGANIZATION

A large company asked a consultant to review their project management issues. It seemed that most project costs were more than expected, were never done on time (if at all), and never accomplished what they were designed to do. Over the phone, they had easily identified more than $500,000 that had been wasted the year before. Obviously, this company was aware of a serious problem worth spending some time, money, and resources to solve.

From an initial review of the company's project list, the consultant found no extreme complexity in the projects that could be causing such a record of inefficiency. He began his search by asking the current project managers two simple questions: How are projects planned here and how are they approved? Here are some responses he got:

- "How are projects planned here? Well, they more evolve. Most of the time, we don't know what we want to do until we start the project and—you know management—they are always changing their minds."
- "How are they approved? You have to understand that we have micro-management here. Management wants infinite detail and then every little detail needs to be approved and re-approved! In other words, you never really get an approval."

- "No one believes the numbers. I spend all my time defending the numbers as the best results I have at that point."
- "We don't have the luxury to plan around here. Every project I've been given should have been done yesterday!"
- "Management doesn't understand. Project management is treated more like an art form than a science or management function. Because they can't understand what it really is, getting any kind of approval is touchy."

The consultant continued his search by asking approving management two different questions: When asking for approval, what kind of project information do they get and what kind of information would they like to get?

- "We're lucky to get an estimate of cost and a completion date. As a starter, those would be nice to know."
- "It's all over the map. Some projects have more details than I want to know and others are so sketchy you can't make a decision. I guess I'd like it somewhere in the middle."
- "I just want numbers. Tell me how much it will cost and when it will be done. Oh...and it would be real nice if they stuck to the cost and date!"
- "To tell you the truth, I'm really never sure what the project is going to accomplish. Sure, I know what we think we want to do but somehow it is never really entrenched in the project information. Do you know what I mean?"
- "You have to understand that project people are a little weird. They're technical folks. I'm sure this is why the information we get is often not what we need. It's kind of like, 'you can't get there from here.' "

Not even having completed his first day of investigation, the consultant already knew the source of the problem. As he told the senior manager, "You don't have a standardized approach to project management. If you did and your project people were trained on it, more than ninety percent of your project woes would simply go away."

"You know that after only a half-day?" he was asked. The fact was, it was just that obvious to someone from the outside. It was not so obvious to anyone on the inside. "How much will that cost?" was the question. In reality, this was a much more complex question than it seems. It was totally dependent upon what process *they* wanted to fix it with. Once an organization identifies this common problem of nonstandardization, this becomes *the* question.

DUFFY

"His desk looked like a bomb had exploded on it. There were pieces of paper everywhere..."

"So I asked... 'What project management process do you use?' He said, 'You're looking at it!' "

SEARCHING FOR ANSWERS

Not having a standardized project management process is a common situation. Surveying most organizations, it may be shocking but most projects are in production without a project management process. Project management seems to just spring up purely by need. If you have projects, you need to manage those projects, right? But just like any other skills that are necessary for effective management, specific skills are necessary for successful project management. While you don't standardize management itself, project management *must* be standardized to be effective.

What does "standardization" really mean? It means that there is an established common process and skill level practice for the management of projects. Standardization is the organization's "way of doing it," with no deviations, substitutions, or alternatives.

Why is project management standardization important to an organization? Simply stated, it removes the unknowns. Ninety-nine percent of projects that go astray do so because unknowns are allowed to exist in the process by which the projects are managed. This is a bold statement but very factual. Dealing with project management in a casual, nonstandardized way cultivates unknowns. They simply grow together. In fact, they become inseparable. Standardization, on the other hand, minimizes unknowns. Minimizing unknowns reduces project problems to a trickle.

Which unknowns does standardizing project management minimize? It minimizes unknowns on all sides of the issue. From a project manager's vantage point, standardization structures the approach and process. It provides a project manager a formal approach that makes it difficult to forget steps or information. It simply makes it harder to fail. Standardization assures that all the necessary information is developed prior to the preliminary or go-ahead approval. Standardization also gives an unproven project manager opportunities to ask questions of his or her project peers. Having one project management system means that the process has been completed many times, which makes communication of important project points and tasks easier for the project manager because all those involved are familiar with the project workings. But, one of the largest advantages for the project manager is that standardization removes the expectation that he or she be brilliant or extremely skilled. It levels the playing field so that new project managers are not at a significant disadvantage due to their limited knowledge or skills proficiency in project management.

From the vantage point of approving management, standardizing the project management process also has significant advantages. To management, the largest advantage is predictability. The process steps are predictable and aligned with the organization's needs and workings. The information on the project is predictable when preliminary or go-ahead approvals are requested. The project information is also always presented in a predictable, known format. Measurement and progress information is in a recognizable and accessible form. Important checks and balances assure that quality and communication are always in place. Even planning is boilerplate. Once time estimates from a previous project are given or needed, budgets for new projects can be requested with a high level of comfort and predictability. Standardization assures that continuous improvement occurs because the process is made better from lessons learned. To management, standardization has so many advantages that it is surprising that project management processes aren't set in cement in every organization. It makes one wonder why the process is so rarely standardized.

THE STANDARDIZATION EFFORT

Merely knowing that standardizing the project management process has significant advantages doesn't get the job done. And an edict from management to standardize the process is not enough either. Successful standardization of the project management process must follow a simple six-step path—concept, plan, train, rollout, monitor, and complete. Establishing a standardized process is, in fact, a project in itself.

Concept: Just as it is important for project management to begin with a clear, simple but thorough project statement, standardizing the process in an organization must begin with the same clarity of concept. The standardization concept must answer the following questions.

- What process or tool will become the standard?
- What benefits will standardization provide?
- Who are the champion and the sponsor?
- Who will lead the effort?
- When will the standardizing effort begin?
- If there are implementation phases, what are they?
- What avenues will be available or used to deal with fear and resistance?
- When will the standardization effort be completed?

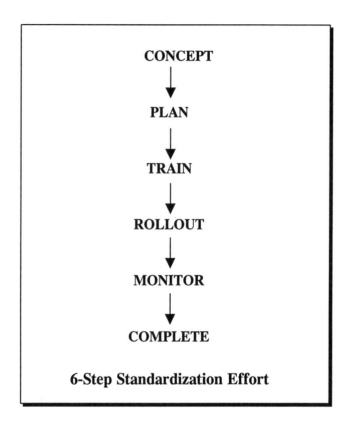

CONCEPT

↓

PLAN

↓

TRAIN

↓

ROLLOUT

↓

MONITOR

↓

COMPLETE

6-Step Standardization Effort

Standardization concepts are usually imposed on the organization under the signature and authority of the top organization manager. In a logical and straightforward manner, each question is addressed.

Plan: Since standardization is itself a project, it is more effective if the standardization plan uses the same tools it is about to place in the organization. Following the same planning steps in establishing standard practices provides a true acid test of the tool or process to be used. If the tool fails in the standardization process, it is time to introduce a more effective tool or process.

The same team-based, heavy input, high communication principles of project management that were introduced in the previous chapters apply to establishing a standardization plan. Breaking down the project into tasks, identifying task durations, assigning responsibilities, and mapping the plan are all critical steps for this process. For many project managers, this will be the first chance they get to see the tools or processes and to work with them. If they make good sense and are easy to follow, you can build organizational confidence in the tools or processes and greatly reduce the impacts of resistance and fear.

Train: Training is critical to standardization. But training shouldn't just be focused at project managers. Training must also include all those who use, approve, liaison with, or are impacted by projects or the project management tool. The following chart summarizes the most important training requirements.

Training that is intended for standardizing anything across an organization always works best if common subjects are taught to mixed audiences, including project support personnel, project management, and upper management. This assures that all participants see the same things, conquer the same fears, and utilize the same forms of communication about the process.

Rollout and Monitor: Rollout follows the implementation of the standardization plan. Task by task, the plan is accomplished in sequence as important project aspects are monitored. These aspects include the schedule itself, those tasks that lie in the critical sequence, resource allocation and accountability, etc. Key tasks and the overall progress should also be measured. This will provide information to everyone impacted by the standardization, including the standardization sponsor and top manager.

Complete: When the standardization plan has been completed and the project management tool or process is implemented organizationwide, it is time for celebration. After all, a significant challenge has been accomplished. With all the rewards that come from standardization, an organization will realize that with successful project management, a celebration is always in order.

Target Group	Project Management Training Requirement
Project Managers	Familiarity with the management tool or process Thorough knowledge and use of the tool or process Obtaining and using project sponsorship Knowing how the tool/process will work in the organization Working in teams and with communication skills Distributing information and forms required for approvals Monitoring and measuring project progress Dealing with project problems
Upper Management	Familiarity with the management tool or process Assigning roles for approving and sponsoring projects Knowing how the tool/process will work in the organization Standardizing approval information and forms Using measurements to gauge project progress
Project Support Personnel	Familiarity with the management tool or process Knowing how the tool/process will work in the organization Working in teams and with communication skills Using measurements to gauge project progress

ORGANIZATIONAL ROADBLOCKS

Implementing any change organizationwide will face some significant roadblocks to success. Even the best standardization plan will fall on its face if these potential roadblocks are not anticipated or planned for. The following is meant to be a summary of change resistance. For a detailed look at change and the resistance it produces, refer to my book *Managing Change for Safety and Health Professionals*, published by Government Institutes.

For our purposes here, it would be easiest to group the potential roadblocks into six major areas—fear, resistance to change, not realizing the true impact, personal preferences, jealousy, and "blink" misconceptions.

Fear: Fear is a basic animal instinct that exists in all of us. In the case of change, it comes mostly from two areas—not knowing what will happen and not feeling competent when new ways are introduced. The first is the fear of the unknown. "I know what you told me but how can I be sure?" Just like the monster that lives in a child's bedroom closet, it is natural to be fearful of what we do not know, don't trust, or cannot see. Effective communication and trust-building techniques are the only balances for fear of the unknown. The second fear source, competency fear, comes from being comfortable doing things the same old way and of not knowing whether we can measure up in the new system. Having a thorough training aspect to your standardization plan will go a long way to removing this type of fear. But you should know that this fear will roam the sidelines of your standardization process until the change has actually happened and the training completed.

Resistance to Change: Resistance and change are hand-and-glove issues. You just don't have change without resistance. This holds true whether the change is negative or positive. The point here is that elimination of resistance is not realistic. Minimizing resistance and keeping it overt (not covert) are your only chances of overcoming it. Often we rationalize that if a change is good then resistance will not follow. This just isn't true. We resist *any* change because it disrupts predictability. Change is always disruptive. Because it is always disruptive, it will always be resisted. Let's look at just one story to illustrate this simple correlation.

A work crew was to be moved from an older facility to a newer one. For most employees, that required an additional 10 minutes of commuting time each day. Care was taken by management to move some of the "character" of the old shop to the new one. Countless crew meetings were held to gather input and information on the move. A senior manager felt that because of the extra 10-minute commute, it would be appropriate to compensate the workers with a travel bonus each week in their pay. This bonus amounted to about $20 per crewmember. Management was sure that the extra compensation would go over like jam on bread. But when the travel bonus was announced, all hell broke loose. One employee had to travel less than the others because of where he lived. Why did he deserve a travel bonus? Another employee had to travel farther than anyone else. Why couldn't he get more of a bonus? One employee's wife would expect dinner out each week because of the extra money. Another just didn't want to have to pay any more taxes.

Dealing with resistance is a challenging issue that requires great skill, patience, communication, and perseverance. The key is to keep the grumbling (and there will be grumbling about *any* change) out in the open and highly verbal. If it is squelched or ignored, it will only go underground and become covert. You can't manage covert communication nor deal with it positively. Covert communication grows and destroys a work group or organization like cancer.

Not Realizing the True Impact: This is mostly a management issue. "I know I said to go ahead with it but I never realized what it would entail or what impact it would have." The root of this potential roadblock is a lack of information, communication, or listening. It is critical that the project manager have all the information on the impact and on what the change will require of management. It is equally important that he or she communicate this information many times and in many different ways. This will help, to some extent, with the listening part.

Personal Preferences: Diversity is one of our strengths, but diversity also means that we have different skills, different ways of looking at things, and different likes and dislikes. What is sweat cream to one is vinegar to another. Project management tools and processes fall prey to this diversity issue. Some people love computerized tools and have little use for the antiquated paper-based systems. Others are afraid of computers, have never developed computer skills, or have no faith in computerized means. Standardization requires that everyone do things the same way. In a way, this is counter to diversity, but through the sameness you gain so much. Allowing the standardized process or tool to become the visible and expected backbone of project management, while still allowing individual project managers to add personal appendages, tools, aids, etc., will help to solve this potential roadblock.

Jealousy: This is as old as the Book of Genesis—remember the story Cain and Abel? "It's your idea so I hate it." "You're getting all the credit so I'm against it." "You've always been the 'golden boy' so I'll drag my feet and make things miserable for you." It's an old story but one that we cannot forget when trying to standardize a project management tool or process into an organization. Some people, even important or higher ranked people, will become roadblocks due to personal jealousies. This is where upper management sponsorship is critical. When jealousy is the root of resistance, power is the only way to remove it.

The "Blink" Misconception: This is one of my favorite roadblocks to talk about. Worded, it would sound like this: "We are now two months into this implementation. I was expecting a much shorter (say...instantaneous) time frame." No matter what your standardization plan and timetable sets up, people have the tendency to ignore time and expect instant success—blink, it's one way, blink it's another. This "blink" misconception can become a significant roadblock if the road to successful implementation is longer than someone (of importance) thought it should be. A helpful hint for minimizing this roadblock is to, first, keep the implementation time span as short as possible. Second, make sure the map (timeline) is always visible from beginning concept to completion.

SUMMARY

It is impossible—or very difficult at best—to manage projects when every process is done differently. This is the same problem when dealing with a lot of projects, each managed by using different tools or processes, with different levels of skills, with different visibility of issues and progress, etc. At best nonstandardized project management is a drain of valuable resources. At worst, it's a nightmare, draining many dollars and depleting many resources.

Standardizing the project management tool or process in an organization just makes good sense. Why would any organization do it differently? Unfortunately, most organizations do not recognize the significant advantages of standardization and choose to deal daily with the mixed bag of methods, personalities, and information. Standardization removes the unknowns, which is what causes 99 percent of projects to go astray, not finish on time, not stay within budget, or never finish at all. Standardization bears significant advantages for both those who manage the projects and those who approve or oversee them.

Successful standardization efforts are run like projects themselves— after all, they *are* projects. Begin with building a clear concept of the standardization effort. Then build a detailed project plan, move to thorough training, and into rollout. During rollout, monitor important aspects and display visual measurements of the effort. At completion, encourage the organization to celebrate its successful efforts.

Potential roadblocks to standardization need to be identified early and preventive plans need to be employed. Preventive strategies include having a thorough training package in your individual plan, using effective communication, having alternative pathways, building trust, expecting resistance, keeping feedback welcome and in the open, allowing personal "attachments" to the standardized process or tool, and keeping the timeline constantly visible and unavoidable. Once a project management process has been successfully standardized, project managers will have an effective means of planning and implementing projects in the future.

8

A PROJECT MANAGEMENT CASE STUDY

The following case study was a Phase I efficiency evaluation project performed at a midsize manufacturing facility in the Midwest. The focus of the efficiency evaluation was toward overhead staffing and processes, primarily in administrative functions. Outside consulting resources that specialized in efficiency evaluations were used. Using this expertise, not only could the myopia of an inside evaluation be avoided but current ideas that were shaping other businesses could also be considered.

The company was very profitable. Management, however, had identified that short-term reversals were probable as projections foresaw steady, if not decreasing, product costs for the following three to five years. A project was undertaken to reduce the overhead costs and thereby place the company in a more advantageous economic position.

The project management tool used in this case study was chosen because it provided visibility of each project management phase and step. It is important to note that from this first phase efficiency evaluation many other implementation phases would arise. These efficiency implementations are not included in this case study due to the number of different projects that came for the study (12) and the extended nature of those implementations (to 4 years in length).

THE OVERHEAD EFFICIENCY EVALUATION PROJECT

During a strategic planning session, the Management Committee of XYZ Company was provided with the following strategic forecast.

Year	World Price of Product	Sales	Profit	Margin
Previous	$38.38	$135M	$16.4M	12.1%
Current	$37.97	$141M	$17.1M	12.1%
Next (First)	$38.00	$140M	$17M	12.1%
Second	$37.75	$140M	$15M	10.7%
Third	$37.50	$141M	$14M	9.9%
Fourth	$36.75	$140M	$10M	7.1%
Fifth	$36.25	$140M	$ 8M	5.7%

The following analysis of expenses provided valuable insight for the management Committee's evaluation of the situation (the analysis has been greatly simplified).

Year	Production Costs	Facility Costs	Administrative Costs
Previous	$76.4M	$12.6M	$29.6M
Current	$76.8M	$13.9M	$33.2M
Next (1st)	$77M	$11M	$35M
Second	$76.5M	$11.5M	$37M
Third	$76M	$12M	$39M
Fourth	$76M	$14M	$40M
Fifth	$76M	$14M	$42M

From this analysis, it was evident that production costs were supporting the decreasing world price for the product; however, administrative costs were escalating at an alarming pace ($29.6M to $42M = 8.4% Annual Growth Rate). This data provided the company justification for the overhead efficiency evaluation and recommendation project.

A project team was identified, sponsored, and empowered to develop the project plan for management's review and approval. The project team was comprised of the following persons (real names have not been used):

Project Team

Team Leader and Project Manager   Mike Tesh, Quality Manager

Team Sponsor (Not sitting on Team)   J. C. Wright, President and CEO

Team Members:	Purchasing	Sue Stanton
	Controller	Fred Crandall
	Marketing	Nathan Moore
	Engineering	John Thompson
	Human Resources	Connie Franklin
	Safety/Environment.	Tom Collinsworth
	Quality	Joanne Jammison
	MIS	Foster Collins
	Production	Thomas Spelling
	Maintenance	George Quick

Project Management Phase I: Concept and Approvals

Step 1: Identify Project Concept, Major Goals and Risks
Developing a Project Statement:

1. **Result:** What is the end result or accomplishment of the project? (Be Specific, e.g., Implement a program, build a building, install a piece of equipment.)

   Identify administrative improvements for Phase II Project implementation.

2. **Budget:** How much will it cost *or* how much budget is allocated?

   Budget Estimate for outside consultant = $500,000

3. **Time:** When does the project have to be done?

   It is desired that Phase I be completed by June 15 so that improvements can be presented at the Summer Management Committee meeting.

4. Combine information from 1-3 above into a clearly worded Project Statement.

Project Statement:

Identify administrative improvements by June 15 for $500,000.

5. Value: In what way(s) will this project provide documentable value to the organization?

- *Hold or reverse administrative cost increases*
- *Return $28M to profit, other improvement projects or building market advantage over 5 years*
- *Decrease administrative function time in support of organization*

6. Risks: What are the risks to the project and the organization? (List)

Organization:
- *Fewer administrative personnel (Downsize Issues)*
- *Disruption of current administrative processes and services to organization*
- *Potentially more dependence on automated or outside resources*
- *Potential changes to management systems*
- *Manpower expense in support of improvement phases*

Project:
- *Legal issues surrounding consulting contract*
- *Management system resistance and interference*
- *Production resistance to improvements*
- *Lack of support and involvement by administrative personnel (Risk of job loss concerns)*
- *Not being able to find or contract outside consultant*

[I:B]

Project Management Phase I: Concept and Approvals

Step 2: Identify Project Objectives and Constraints

1. Objectives: Once completed, what will be the *measurable* benefits? (What must the project be able to do?)

   - *Identify multiple improvement projects across all areas of administration*
   - *Calculations of improvement costs will hold or decrease projected administrative cost escalation ($\geq$ $28M over 5 years)*
   - *Provide future administrative staffing estimates*
   - *Identify administrative process changes and associated resource needs*

2. Constraints: What limiting factors must also successfully be met?

   Time limitations:

   > *Must be compete by June 15 for committee meeting*

   Resource limitations:

   > *Administrative personnel time in support of this project must not negatively impact service to organization*

   Conflicts:

   > *Project must not impede progress on concurrent MIS project for computerizing purchasing process*

   Codes/Standards/Permits/etc.:

   > *None*

   Others:

[I:C]

Project Management Phase I: Concept and Approvals

Step 3: Obtain Preliminary Approval for the Project

1. "Package" the information appropriately and effectively.

What format will be used?

Formal presentation to management team

What information is needed?

Project Management Phase I information
Estimation of required budget
Contractor search listing

2. Who needs this information and what lead-time is best?

Person/Position	by When?
J. C. Wright, President and CEO	*Daily Briefings*
Management committee members	*Feb. 1*
Staff managers	*Feb. 1*
All administration managers	*Feb. 5*
Communicator	*Feb. 5*

[I:D]

3. What is the urgency of the project?

Are approval discussions/meetings/presentations aligned with this urgency?

Yes, CEO daily briefings and management information by Feb. 1

4. What questions can you anticipate and what information do you need to have prepared before time?

Questions:	Needed Information
What outside consultants will you consider?	*Search data*
What preliminary data do you anticipate needing?	*Costs/Processes*
What basis will be used to select consultant?	*Stratified Criteria*
Is break-even the ending criteria or most efficient?	*Team Decision*
Can we do this in-house?	*Survey Information*
Are we missing someone on the project team?	*Brainstorm Prior*
How are decisions going to be made—by consensus?	*Team Decision*

[I:E]

Project Management Phase I: Concept and Approvals

Step 4: Identify the Major Project Elements and Create a Project Map

1. Using small "stickies" identify all the major project elements, put them in order, then number each. (Rule: No more than eight major elements!)

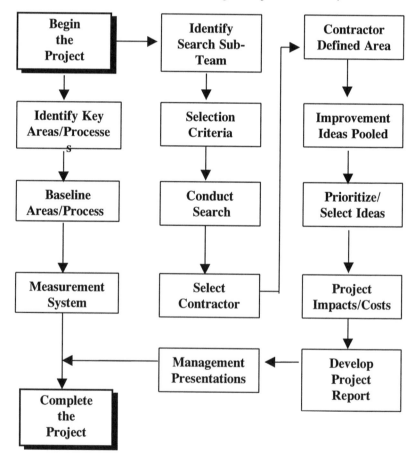

[I:F]

2. Identify all tasks on the vertical Project Work Breakdown Sheet and assign a realistic duration to each task:

3. In the space below, create either a vertical or horizontal project map showing task sequence, dependence, and duration. (**Helpful Hint:** To minimize repetition, use only task numbers from vertical work breakdown.)

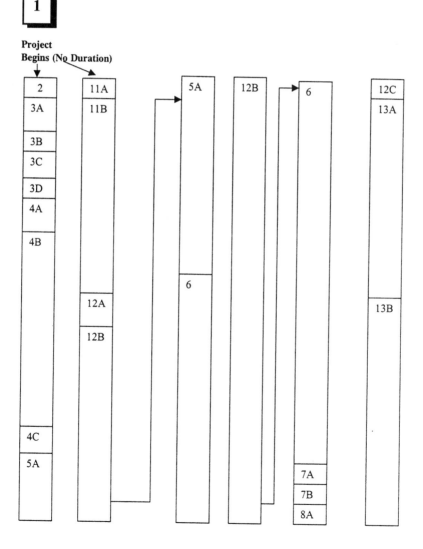

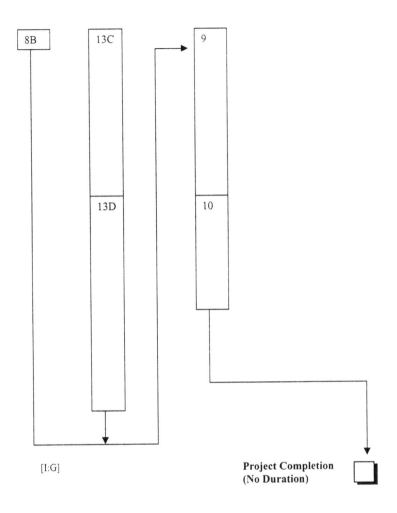

[I:G]

Project Completion
(No Duration)

Project Work Breakdown Sheet

Phase/Task	Duration	Resources	Assignment
1. Begin the Project	-	-	-
2. Identify Search Sub-Team	1 Day	Team	Mike Tesh
3. Develop Selection Criteria	-	-	Nathan Moore
A. Telephone Poll Companies	3 Days	Sub-Team	Moore-Lead
B. Pool All Information	1 Day	Sub-Team	Moore-Lead
C. Select Selection Criteria	2 Days	Sub-Team	Moore-Lead
D. Review Criteria with Full Team	1 Day	Sub-Team	Moore-Lead
4. Conduct Search	-	-	Nathan Moore
A. Send RFPs to Contractor List	1 Day	Purchasing	SueStranton
B. Receive Proposals	10 Days	Purchasing	SueStranton
C. Measure Against Criteria	2 Days	Team	Moore-Lead
5. Select Contractor	-	-	Nathan Moore
A. Contract Negotiations	10 Days	Council	Harvey Kemp
6. Contractor Defined Area	60 Days	Contractor	TBD
7. Improvement Ideas Pooled	-	-	Fred Crandall
A. Divide Ideas by Area	1 Day	Team	Crandall-Lead
B. Divide Areas by Impact	1 Day	Team	Crandall-Lead
8. Prioritize/Select Ideas	-	-	Fred Crandall
A. Develop Cut-Off Points	1 Day	Team	Crandall-Lead

B. Apply Points to Pools	1 Day	Team	Crandall-Lead
9. Develop Project Report	10 Days	Team	Mike Tesh
10. Management Presentations	5 Days	Team	Mike Tesh
11. Identify Key Areas/Processes	-	-	Foster Collins
A. Divide Administration Areas	1 Day	Team	Collins-Lead
B. Identify Processes in Each Area	10 Days	Team	Collins-Lead
12. Baseline Areas/Processes	-	-	Foster Collins
A. Select Area Helpers	2 Days	Team	Collins-Lead
B. Process Map Each Process	60 Days	Team	Collins-Lead
C. Collect All Process Maps	1 Day	Team	Collins-Lead
13. Measurement Systems	-	-	Foster Collins
A. Select Key Issues in Processes	10 Days	Team	Collins-Lead
B. Develop Measures	10 Days	Team	Collins-Lead
C. Develop Visual Systems	10 Days	Team	Collins-Lead
D. Create Visual Measurements	10 Days	Team	Collins-Lead
14. Complete the Project	-	-	-

[I:H]

Project Management Phase I: Concept and Approvals

Step 5: **Identify Project Resource Needs**

Using the Project Work Breakdown Sheet, identify the appropriate resources for each task.

Project Management Phase I: Concept and Approvals

Step 6: Obtain the Go-Ahead Approval for the Project

1. Identify the essential outcomes for project success:

Budget: *$500,000*

Resources: *Administration Helpers*
Team Member Time Cleared
Council to Aid in Contracting

Time: *128 Days*

Sponsorship: *CEO's Unwavering Support*

Contract: *None*

[I:I]

2. Plan your approval-seeking meeting/presentation:

Who needs to be there?
Staff Management
Management Committee Members
J. C. Wright, President and CEO

What presentation/information conveying tools will you use?
Project Packets
Packet Summaries on Slides

When is the meeting/presentation?
January 15

What specific information do you need to provide?
Project Packets

What questions can you anticipate and what additional information do you need to have?

(None Additional)

[I:J]

Project Management Phase II: Planning and Analysis

Step 1: Assign Project Jobs and Tasks

Using the Project Work Breakdown Sheet, assign specific responsibility to each task and oversight/management responsibility to each major project element. (**Helpful Hint:** Assign responsibilities to persons not teams or departments.)

Project Management Phase II: Planning and Analysis

Step 2: Establish Critical Sequence of Tasks and Dependent Tasks

Using the project map completed for Phase I, Step 4, Number 3, add up all possible task sequences from project beginning to completion. Highlight the one sequence route that has the fewest days. This is the Critical Sequence.

Project Management Phase II: Planning and Analysis

Step 3: Develop and Chart Project Schedule

1. Fold the Project Chart Sheet at the left border and tape it to the right border of the Project Work Breakdown Sheet.

2. At the top of the Project Chart Sheet record the appropriate calendar dates or days.

3. **Gantt Chart:** Beginning with Task 2A, record each task's duration vertically using line or block legend means.

4. Highlight the Critical Sequence of Tasks.

Project Chart Sheet — Page 1 of 12

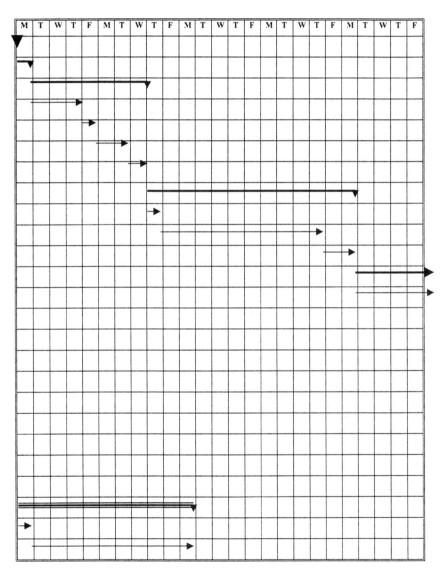

Project Chart Sheet — Page 2 of 12

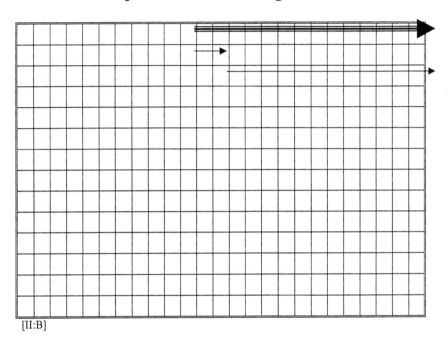

[II:B]

Project Chart Sheet — Page 3 of 12

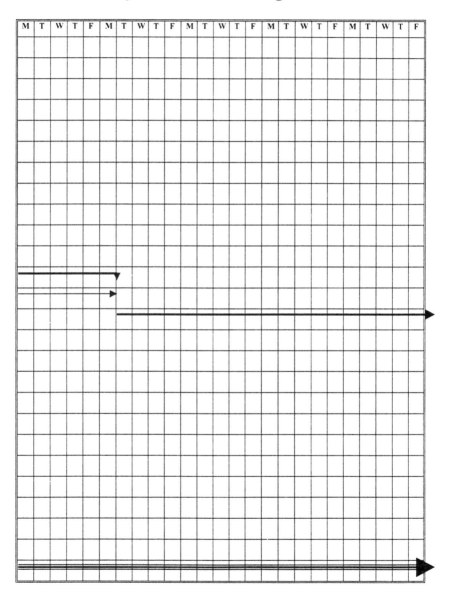

Project Chart Sheet — Page 4 of 12

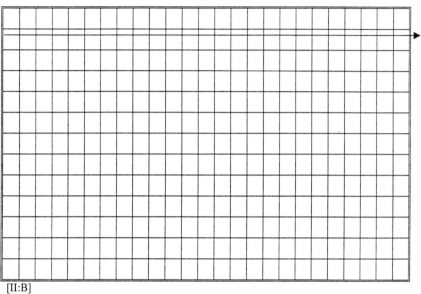

[II:B]

Project Chart Sheet — Page 5 of 12

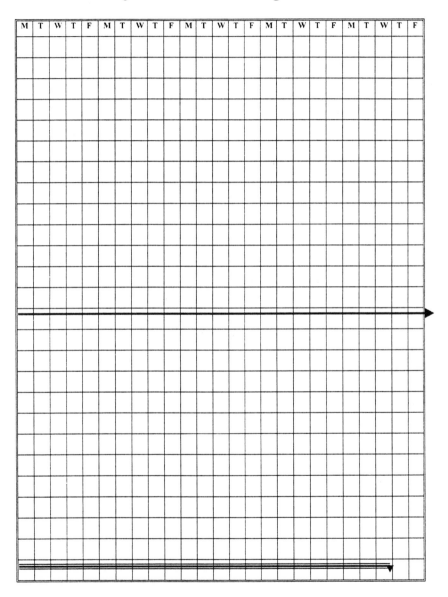

Project Chart Sheet — Page 6 of 12

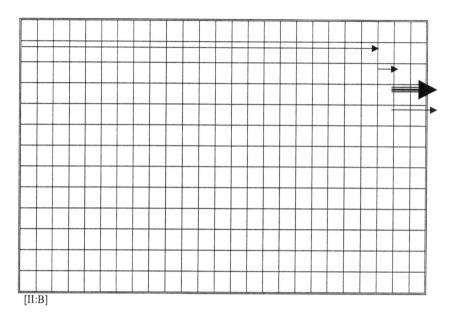

[II:B]

Project Chart Sheet — Page 7 of 12

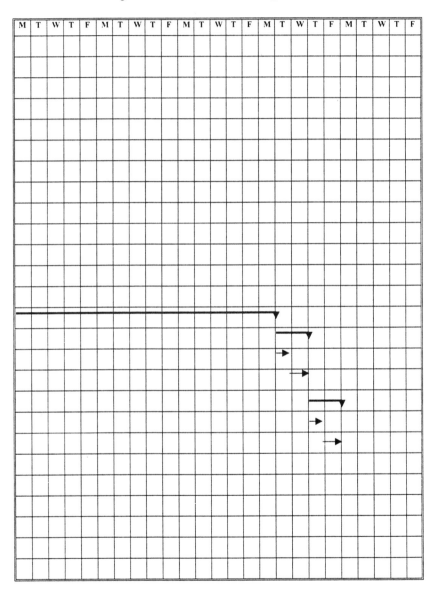

Project Chart Sheet — Page 8 of 12

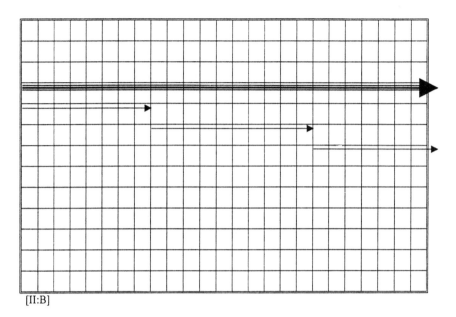

[II:B]

Project Chart Sheet — Page 9 of 12

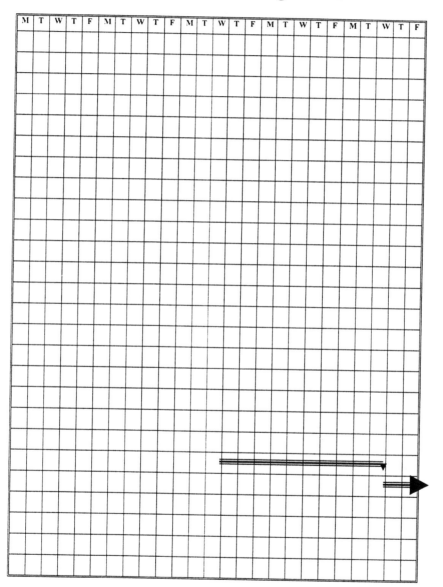

Project Chart Sheet — Page 10 of 12

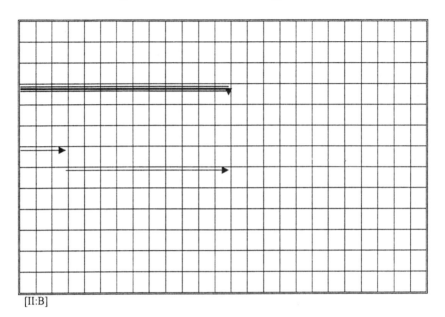

[II:B]

Project Chart Sheet — Page 11 of 12

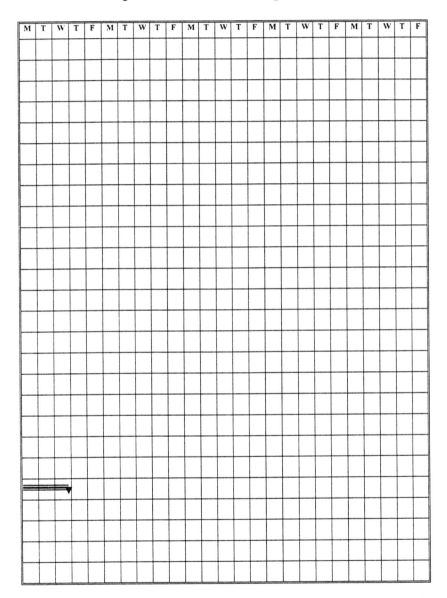

Project Chart Sheet — Page 12 of 12

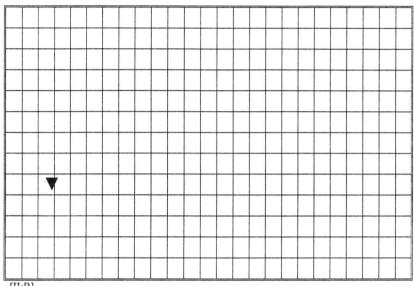

[II:B]

Project Management Phase II: Planning and Analysis

Step 4: Schedule Resource Deployment

Identify key resources people to be included in this step.

All Project Team Members and Sponsor
Paul Pierpoint, Purchasing Manager
Fran Lopez, Engineering Manager
Laurie Smith, Human Resources Manager
Hugh Caston, Safety and Environmental Manager
Tom Freed, Marketing Manager
Linda Polla, MIS Manager
Rick Chang, Production Manager
Carlos Rodriguez, Maintenance Manager
Harvey Kemp, Council
Contractor (When Identified and Contracted)

Helpful Hints for successful Project Managers:

1. Include key resource people in planning discussions.

2. Share a copy of the final project plan with key resource people.

3. Make sure pre-task communication is adequate for importance of task and schedule.

4. Include post-task communications for collecting lessons-learned information.

[II:C]

Project Management Phase II: Planning and Analysis

Step 5: **Identify Potential Problems and Make Prevention Plans**

1. Using the Problem Prevention Sheet, use the following criteria to identify potential problem tasks.

   - List tasks, critical or noncritical, that require the most resources or are the most complex.
   - List tasks that have the tightest assigned durations.
   - List tasks that are critical to more than one dependent task downstream.
   - List tasks that are accomplished by resources totally outside your control or influence.
   - List tasks that are assigned to resources who, in the past, have been less than dependable.
   - List tasks that are assigned to resources who are or are apparently over-booked or overworked.
   - List tasks that are led by members of management by the project management team who are less dependable, overly committed, or busy.

2. For each, determine what could cause the problem.
3. Identify a simple but specific prevention plan for each.
4. Stratify the potential problem task list by severity of outcome (high versus low).
5. Stratify the high severity potential problem tasks by probability of occurrence (high versus low).
6. Transfer preventive actions of high probability/high severity potential problem tasks to project plan.
7. Identify possible triggers that can be used early for prevention plan implementation.

[II:D]

Problem Prevention Sheet

List of Potential Problem Tasks	Cause of Problem	Prevention Plan
11B: Identify processes in each area	Lack of training	Include 1 day of training at task start
12B: Process map each process	Lack of training	Include 2 days of training at task start
13B: Develop measures	Lack of experience	Use Tom Rich as task mentor
13C: Develop visual systems	Lack of computer aids	Get support from MIS
10: Management presentations	Scheduling problems	Schedule a month out over CEO's signature

[II:E]

Project Management Phase II: Planning and Analysis

Step 6: Identify Potential Opportunities for Making Up Ground

1. Using the Opportunity Planning Sheet, use the following criteria to identify potential opportunity tasks.

- List tasks, critical or noncritical, that require the least resources or are the least complex.
- List tasks that have the most liberal assigned durations.
- List tasks that can be done ahead of schedule.
- List tasks that are accomplished by you or by resources that are totally under your control or influence.
- List tasks that will get no attention or are really window dressing.
- List tasks that are assigned to resources who have the reputation of getting work done early.
- List tasks that are assigned to resources who are underbooked and underworked.
- List tasks that are lead by members of management or of the project management team who are always dependable or not busy

2. Identify a simple but specific plan for taking advantage of each.
3. Stratify the potential opportunity task list by the amount of time each could make up (high versus low).
4. Stratify the high makeup potential opportunity tasks by probability of occurrence (high versus low).
5. Transfer opportunity actions of high probability/high makeup potential opportunity tasks to project plan.
6. Identify key potential problem tasks upstream that could trigger the need to focus on an opportunity task.

[II:F]

Opportunity Planning Sheet

List of Potential Opportunity Tasks	Opportunity Actions
13A: Select key issues in processes	Begin as soon as maps are available
13B: Develop measures	Find measures that will measure multiple processes
13C: Develop visual systems	Poll area businesses
13D: Create visual measurements	Poll area businesses

[II:G]

Project Management Phase III: Project Implementation

Step 1: Begin Implementation
  1. Identify the areas of special attention during project implementation:

   Schedule:
   4 & 5. Contractor search and selection (Contracting)
   6. Contractor defined work and schedule
   11. & 12. Processes and Maps

   Communication:
   5. Contractor selection (Contracting)
   6. Contractor defined work/progress/goals

   Resource Coordination:
   11. & 12. Processes and Maps

   Budget:
   6. Contractor work
   13. Computerization

   Other:

  2. What mechanism(s) will be used to capture lessons for learning?

   Develop and use "Lessons Learned" wall in team meeting room
   Weekly team agenda discussions on lessons learned

[III:A]

Project Management Phase III: Project Implementation

Step 2: Monitor and Measure Progress of the Project

1. List results to resources ratios that will be monitored during the project.

Budget Items:
Expended budget against projected budget spending
Contractor billings against budget and time

Schedule Items:
Progress against schedule
Critical sequence progress against schedule

Problem Items:
Number of unexpected problems
Schedule delays per problem

Opportunity Items:
Days gained from key opportunity tasks

Interface Items:
Total days delayed due to communication failures

Other Items:
None

[III:B]

2. List what will be measured and how.

Measured Ratio	X/Y Axis	Display
Expended budget against projected budget (Two Plotted Lines)	Y: Dollars Spent X: Project Time	Wall and distributed
Critical sequence progress against schedule (Two Plotted Lines)	Y: % Completed X: Project Time	Wall and distributed
Time delays and gains	Y: Days + or - X: Project Time	Wall only

Where will these measures be visible?

Project team meeting room wall
Administration building foyer wall
Central management meeting room wall

How will key management/impacted people be appraised of measures?

Visual on walls
Weekly progress report to management with measures

[III:C]

Project Management Phase III: Project Implementation

Step 3: Evaluate and Modify the Project Plan as Necessary
List the rules you will use for reviewing and modifying the project plan.

1. One day missed constitutes concern *not* panic.
2. Require that leads and subteam leaders advise project team of progress against schedule daily.
3. Delays of more than a day will be reviewed by the project team and appropriate actions taken.

Who will make decisions on modifying the plan?

The project manager as advised by the project team

List plan modifications below.
Contract negotiations required 12 days—no modification, noncritical sequence task.
Identifying processes in each area took 13 days — three days removed from 13.
Measurement Systems
Developing measures required only 6 days—no modification to schedule
Written project report was completed in 8 days — no modification to schedule

[III:D]

Project Management Phase III: Project Implementation

Step 4: Finish the Project

1. List those who must be communicated with when the project is complete.

> *J. C. Wright, President and CEO*
> *Management committee*
> *All staff managers and administration managers*
> *Company communicator*
> *All project team members*

2. Detail your celebration plans.

> *Dinner for all involved in project with spouses at Lion Den Restaurant*
> *J. C. Wright letter of thanks to each involved*
> *Ice cream sundae bar in administration lunchroom for all administration personnel*

[III:E]

Project Management Phase III: Project Implementation

Step 5: Determine Lessons Learned

1. **Capturing:** List all pieces of potential lessons learned information and list on an independent sheet.

2. **Compiling:** Group information into broad project categories.

3. **Dividing:** Separate the listed information under each broad project category into big issues and little issues. Put the major issues on the Lessons Learned Table.

4. **Analyzing:** Determine the probable cause (singular) for each big lesson.

5. **Brainstorming:** Identify the most likely prevention action.

6. **Documenting:** Transfer the information to your ongoing planning schedule.

[III:F]

Lessons Learned Table

Information Captured	Most probable Cause	Planned Preventive Action
Long contract negotiations	New contract language	Plan more time
Identifying processes slow	Team dynamics struggled	Add team dynamics training
Developing measures fast	MIS support and help	Tuck MIS in early in plan
Report done early	Developed in stages	Communication critical
Management got nervous	Fear of impact/findings	Better communication
Rumors in administration	Fear of impact/findings	Weekly admin. updates
Communicator slow	Busy	Make info easier and visual
Some team difficulties	Personality clashes	Team dynamics training
Too many disruptive questions	Didn't understand format	Standardize project process

[III:G]

Project Management Phase III: Project Implementation

Step 6: Project Close Out and Documentation

1. Review the project information and be sure that everything is complete.

2. List all key people involved in the project.

   Project Team:
   - S. Stranton, Buyer – Purchasing
   - F. Crandall, Controller
   - N. Moore, Product Specialist – Marketing
   - J. Thompson, Principle Engineer – Engineering
   - C. Franklin, HR Specialist — Human Resources
   - T. Collinsworth, Senior Safety Specialist — S&E
   - J. Jammison, Quality Auditor – Quality
   - F. Collins, Network Specialist – MIS
   - T. Spelling, Process Engineer – Production
   - G. Quick, PM Scheduler – Maintenance
   - M. Tesh, Quality Manager (Team Leader)
   - J. C. Wright, President & CEO (Sponsor)

3. Applicable notes and after-thoughts on the project:

   The project had farther-reaching impacts and information than originally conceived in project design. Process identification and mapping provided great information on administration processes and allowed improvements aside from this project. Having heavy administrative input and involvement improved the esprit de corps of the administrative departments. Team abilities of all improved. And, the visual measurement systems will be continued to add documentation of the administrative system value to the organization.

This project checklist documents the steps and approach used to manage this project. The checklist solved a lot of mental and process problems for the project management team. Because this project management process was formalized, important steps throughout a complex project were not missed. The project team was allowed to plan for learning and to impart what they learned back into the process. This case study not only documents a successful project management process, but also indicates where the project management process and skills can be further improved.

SUMMARY

This case study certainly does not suggest that the provided manual checklist approach to project management is the only one that works. It was very successful in this example, but other project management tools and processes can be just as successfully used.

There are three important points, however, that successful project managers and project approvers must take from this case study. First, it is important to use formal project management tools or processes. There is too much potential for waste and derailing if a structured process is not used. Second, to assure knowledge, familiarity, and trust throughout the organization, the project management process or tool needs to be standardized. And third, there are a lot of skills that need to be taught, trained for, and included in a project's plan. These skills include process or tool familiarization, team skills, mentoring use, and basic skills pertaining to the particular project. In this case study, process-mapping and team skills were important.

9

FROM WASTE TO EFFICIENCY

We began this book with a rather bleak look at traditional project management where skills are questionable, waste is high, frustration is common, real approvals are rare, and standardization for efficiency is only a dream. Most who are employed in organizations where project management makes up a large portion of the work, will not argue with this bleak description of traditional project management. But one has to ask, if our traditional process of project management is that bad, and yet it is such an important process for adding value and minimizing waste, why isn't the situation different? Good question. Fortunately, it is an easy one to answer.

Project management continues in its traditional pattern for four reasons. First, most people do not recognize that project management is a learned skill. It is still thought that project management proficiency is just an outgrowth of a technical degree program. Actually, project management skills are not taught, or even addressed, in almost all of the technical education programs in our nation's colleges and universities. So where do these project management skills that form our traditional patterns come from? They come from everywhere. They are a hodge-podge of individual experiences, skills and non-skills, knowledge and ignorance, and mixing of "someone else's" thinking. Project management skills are like a collection of junk in the garage. A new idea is conceived or an upper manager makes a comment about project management and it gets moved into the project management garage for storage and use.

Second, there is an organizational (and management) acceptance of the problems and wastes associated with traditional project management. We capitulate to inefficiency of the traditional approach, thinking that this is "the way it is." Think of this absurdity in a different way. Imagine management, and our business world for that matter, conceding that accounting was racked with errors and wastes, just because that's "the way it is." Can you imagine the problems that would arise from a company not knowing how much money it is making or losing? Can you imagine the stockholders report of that company? Can you imagine the IRS accepting this highly wasteful accounting practice in any company or especially allowing it to exist across the country? You can't imagine it because it wouldn't happen. We do not have the same acceptance of wastes and problems when it comes to accounting as we do with project management. There is obviously a paradigm problem here.

Third, the magnitude of this waste via traditional project management is not often recognized or brought into the light. It was estimated that wasted time and money in American project management, however, could easily total twice the peak annual addition to the national debt. Now that's pretty sobering, isn't it? But, we don't recognize the size of the waste and the total costs to our companies, organizations, and country because these costs enter the room in small percentage budget increases or in requests for adding a few extra days to the schedule. "We need an approval for an 8 percent cost overrun." Or, "The project will be done on time if you allow me another week to get it done." These nickel-and-dime wastes obscure the big picture, which is the sum of all those little wastes. Those wastes add up to big numbers...very big numbers.

And fourth, project management is a "technical thing" and management does not consider it to be their function to standardize or mess with "technical skills." This is an American management paradigm. We manage the balance sheet (accounting); we manage the hiring, salaries, benefits (personnel). We manage the procurement process. We manage the production, service provision, and maintenance functions. But these functions are not viewed as technical things, which somehow cannot be managed like real "business things." This, of course, is hogwash!

In reality, *we* in safety and health also allow this traditional approach to project management to exist. We seldom stop to see if there is a better way of doing it. It takes real paradigm shifts—new, creative thinking that is so different from traditional thinking and which often must come from outside that particular field or area. Free and independent thinkers who come up with the new paradigms aren't invested in the old ways of doing and thinking. They simply don't know any better. They haven't learned and conformed to the traditional "rules." This isn't always the case but is true in a vast majority of cases. Just as the alarm clock that sits by your bed rings to awaken you to a new day, I hope this book to be a paradigm alarm clock. Ringing, it says, "It's time to wake up and change some things!"

Change, of course, begins individually and, when proven successful, grows outward. Project management skills, processes, and standardization are all ready to undergo this change.

A PROCESS FOR SUCCESSFUL PROJECT MANAGEMENT

We've taken a detailed look into a three-phase, eighteen-step process for project management. Phase I includes developing the project concept and moves through a two-step, preliminary and go-ahead approval process. This first phase of successful project management sets the stage for everything that comes after. The major deliverables from Phase I are the project statement and objectives, and a cemented identification of the budget, time, and resources necessary for the project.

Phase II of successful project management is the planning and analysis phase. Responsibilities are assigned, the critical sequence of tasks is identified, the project is charted into a visual format, resources are scheduled, and problems and opportunities are identified, allowing avoidance or capitalization efforts to be moved into the project plan. Just as Phase I could be called the identification and go-ahead phase,

Phase II could be termed the mapping and scheduling phase, where all the meat is attached to the bones.

Phase III begins with project implementation—putting the plan into action. This is the most visible, tangible portion of project management. But, as with the other phases, there are other important aspects of project implementation to remember, including monitoring important project aspects and performance, measuring key indicators, and evaluating and modifying the project plan as necessary. After project implementation is finished, determining the lessons learned provides for continual improvement to the project management process. Getting all the paperwork completed assures project completion and close out.

The project management phases and steps appear in the chart on the next page.

The project management checklist approach discussed in this book and used in the case study is derived from this eighteen-step approach. Other tools or processes can be used; however, they tend to focus only on their particular advantages. Often times, just focusing on the positive elements of any process causes us to miss important details that can make or break a process or system. That's why the eighteen-step approach to project management is included. It evolved from a combination of many different tools and project management processes, taking the best parts and leaving the shrubbery and the 'bells and whistles" behind.

KEY SKILLS INVENTORY

Project management skills do not stand alone; they form an important part of a skill tapestry in which many skills are interwoven. Without these other skills, everything unravels and project management is not whole. These other skills include team building and team dynamic skills, working effectively with people skills, communication skills, and resource coordination skills.

PROJECT MANAGEMENT – PHASES AND STAGES

Phase I: Concept and Approvals

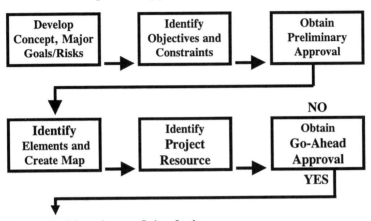

Phase II: Planning and Analysis

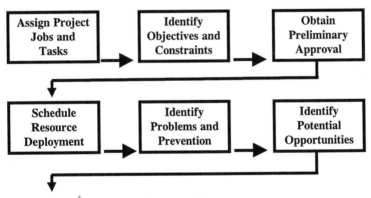

Phase III: Project Implementation

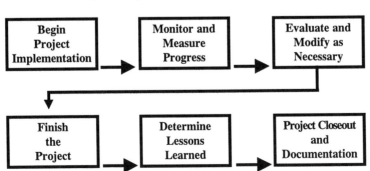

Team Building and Team-Dynamics Skills: There is little room in the project management world for supermen or superwomen. Project management is a team dynamic in the most literal sense. Successful completion of the project and its objectives depends on a number of people working together in a coordinated fashion to accomplish a complex series of tasks. Like any team in sports, wins or loses are based on the ability to excel as a team. Project management depends on this same team dynamic.

Generally, project management teams are created for the duration of the project and are disbanded at its completion. Additionally, depending on the complexity or length of the project, the team can enlarge and shrink during the life of a project. This is dependent upon specialized players who contribute for a particular period or phase of the project and then are no longer needed. This flexibility requires a successful project manager with good team-building and dynamics skills. Without them, the entire effort becomes a one-person show, severely lacks cohesion and coordination, and usually fails totally or in part of the project or objectives.

Working Effectively with People Skills: A project has tentacles that reach into various skill or resource areas that are necessary for the successful completion of the project. These resource areas may include engineering help, drafting or design experts, outside contractors, department or support management, purchasing and accounting personnel, human resource specialists, or quality control professionals. Depending on the project and the various skills or resources necessary, project management requires working with a lot of other people. Obviously, having effective skills for working with people is very important to successful project management.

Good Communication Skills: From the opening volley to the final shot of the project, communication is critical. A successful project manager must explain the project idea effectively to concept people, upper management, dependent management, project sponsors, project team members, resource people, specialists, and area personnel. Actually, communication is the fuel that drives or starves the project.

You can be exceptionally skilled in project planning and scheduling, but if your plans and schedules are not effectively communicated to others, you might as well not have invested the energy. Nothing will get done, at lease not effectively or on time without communication. Communication skills are essential to successful project management.

Resource Coordination Skills: Resource coordination skills are very specialized. Coordination of varied resources is like spinning many plates on vertical sticks all at the same time. The trick is to keep them all spinning at a sufficient rotational velocity to keep them up. If they lose speed, they wobble, fall off the stick and break. Resource coordination is all about keeping the plates spinning and on top of the sticks.

DUFFY

"My boss told me that he never saw a project completed on time and under budget..."

"I just said 'Thanks.' Then I made a note to bring this exchange up during my annual performance evaluation!"

APPLYING A SUCCESSFUL PROCESS

Having taken on a new assignment, a colleague of mine was given a career-building or career-destroying opportunity. A large project was conceived that no one else wanted because it had a very high chance of failure. This same project concept had been attempted twice earlier without success. Those who were "chosen" to lead the previous failures were either no longer with the company or had been "cubby-holed" deep within the organization. Everyone knew the history. That's why no one else wanted it.

My colleague friend, however, is an optimist. He finds beauty in weeded lots and an opportunity in near-certain failure. This project was no exception. His mission was to define, implement, and sell a new, more effective way of providing and coordinating safety and environmental efforts throughout a large, multinational conglomerate corporation. Being a large conglomerate, the company faced many challenges caused by facility diversity. Being a multinational company, there were many cultural barriers that the project manager would need to address successfully. Being a large corporation, the company had plenty of political barriers he would also have to negotiate. This project was a considerable challenge. But he was undaunted because he was confident he had developed very good project management and communication skills to carry him through.

He began the project by getting a very clear understanding from upper management of what the project goals and objectives would be and a clear idea of what time and budget constraints could be expected. He decided to divide the project into a two-team endeavor. The first team would be comprised of "movers and shakers" from inside and outside the corporation who had the necessary political clout and contacts. This would be his Project Concept Team and it would lead the way to project go-ahead approval. The members of this team would come mostly from the recommendations of sponsoring management. The second team, the Project Management Team, would be responsible for the planning and implementation phases and would be comprised of people inside the corporation who were creative thinkers and good communicators and who had reputations for being innovative and successful. He and the boss, it was decided, would select the Project Management Team.

He detailed his project approach in a formal request for a preliminary concept-developing budget. Working through his boss and vice president, he was granted the budget he needed and began to seek recommendations for the Project Concept Team members from upper management.

Recognizing that project anonymity could be his worse enemy, especially if the project or upper management support faltered, he began an active communication program, which included regular e-mail messages to management and department staff, and update sheets posted on department bulletin boards and near water coolers. He began talking about and selling his project at every opportunity, including at lunch and breaks. He took his role as project champion very seriously.

The Project Concept Team was named within a month. A meeting was arranged at a centrally located place within the next month. It took them two days to come together as at team and develop the project statement and objectives. These were e-mailed to his boss and vice president for review and comment. Because the project manager did his homework and found out firsthand what upper management wanted in the project concept, what the team developed was aligned with management's original intentions. A preliminary approval came back by noon of the next day.

The third and fourth days were spent developing a project map and identifying what resources would be necessary. The work was done so well that they celebrated by playing golf on the fifth day. The project manager kept meticulous notes of each day's work, summarized them nightly, and e-mailed them to his boss. Developing the materials for the presentation was easy but it took almost a month to schedule the presentation/approval meeting. With an important project like this, a very professional, formal presentation with attendee packets was in order. This gave the project manager plenty of time to prepare the presentation materials the way he wanted them to be.

The project proposal was presented before the Corporate Management Committee. In less than 45 minutes, the go-ahead approval with resource and budget commitments were given. The project manager moved on to assembling the Project Management Team so that Phase II could begin.

Facility and cultural diversity was the first qualifying criteria used to make the potential list of members for the Project Management Team. Thirty-seven names were on the first list. While maintaining diversity, creative thinkers were highlighted. This narrowed the list to twelve.

Those who were known for their excellence and successful work further narrowed the list to six, but that number was increased to nine to maintain diversity. Three additional members were added from critical resources and customer areas including a facility line manager, a corporate upper management liaison, and a human resources representative.

A two-week meeting was scheduled to work through the steps of Phase II. The training department was brought in as a project resource to spend the first day teaching team dynamics skills and bringing the Project Management Team to cohesion. Day two was spent sharing experiences, both from a cultural and individual organizational perspective. At the end of the second day, a cohesive team emerged with a very expanded frame of reference. This team was ready to begin their important planning process.

By the end of the first week, 80 to 90 percent of the plan and schedule was planned. As before, at the end of each day's work, the project manager e-mailed the day's summary to his boss. This was an important aspect of the communication process. The team chose to work through the weekend, but had to take a day-long break after day seven for rest. By the tenth day, key resources were identified and scheduled, the potential problems were anticipated in the plan, and preliminary opportunities were identified. A second, reflective day of rest was scheduled. By the end of the second week, a complete project plan and schedule was developed and a Project Implementation Team identified. This team would be a subteam of the Project Management Team, comprised of members who were geographically near to the corporate offices. The other Project Management Team members would be apprised weekly by e-mail. At this point, the project was one month ahead of schedule and below projected budget by 18 percent.

As an extra measure, the complete plan was presented to the Corporate Management Committee, seeking their approval and endorsement. The plan received overwhelming support.

Project implementation was begun in March and completed in September, three months ahead of the original time restraints stated by upper mangement. The budget was 32 percent below the approved amount. More than that, the changes were overwhelmingly accepted in the facilities by both management and other professionals. The changes saved the corporation over $10 million in the first year alone. This project was a tremendous success!

That particular project manager, like his less successful project predecessors, no longer works for that corporation—but for a different reason. Following the successful completion of the project, his boss and vice president offered him a very healthy promotion and raise. But, having the confidence and know-how (and a full lessons learned file), he formed his own company and now does project management work for other corporations. Being a successful project manager provides many rewards.

SUMMARY

Project management skills aren't something anyone is born with; they are learned skills. Interrelated skills such as team building and dynamics, effective communication, people skills, and resource coordination skills are also learned skills. My professional colleague in the above case study used all of those skills very well. Everyone in the company benefited, including management, my colleague, and workers' safety and health. That's a pretty nice result. Had he decided that project management was merely an extension of his regular skills, he probably would have failed and the result would have been very different.

Project management skills are neither rocket science nor brain surgery. Standardizing them in an organization is not a reinvention of the wheel. But, standardization of project management tasks is a critically important effort for an organization that frequently assigns projects to managers. Being successful at project management only takes an acceptance that project management skills are learned skills, and that learning them and standardizing the process is beneficial to the entire organization. It takes a leadership role by those who want to hone their project management skills and improve the overall process.

Leadership skills, too, are not something anyone is born with. But...that's a subject for another book.

INDEX

GOVERNMENT INSTITUTES MINI-CATALOG

PC #	ENVIRONMENTAL TITLES	Pub Date	Price
585	Book of Lists for Regulated Hazardous Substances, 8th Edition	1997	$79
4088	CFR Chemical Lists on CD ROM, 1997 Edition	1997	$125
4089	Chemical Data for Workplace Sampling & Analysis, Single User	1997	$125
512	Clean Water Handbook, 2nd Edition	1996	$89
581	EH&S Auditing Made Easy	1997	$79
587	E H & S CFR Training Requirements, 3rd Edition	1997	$89
4082	EMMI-Envl Monitoring Methods Index for Windows-Network	1997	$537
4082	EMMI-Envl Monitoring Methods Index for Windows-Single User	1997	$179
525	Environmental Audits, 7th Edition	1996	$79
548	Environmental Engineering and Science: An Introduction	1997	$79
578	Environmental Guide to the Internet, 3rd Edition	1997	$59
560	Environmental Law Handbook, 14th Edition	1997	$79
353	Environmental Regulatory Glossary, 6th Edition	1993	$79
562	Environmental Statutes, 1997 Edition	1997	$69
562	Environmental Statutes Book/Disk Package, 1997 Edition	1997	$204
4060	Environmental Statutes on Disk for Windows-Network	1997	$405
4060	Environmental Statutes on Disk for Windows-Single User	1997	$135
570	Environmentalism at the Crossroads	1995	$39
536	ESAs Made Easy	1996	$59
515	Industrial Environmental Management: A Practical Approach	1996	$79
4078	IRIS Database-Network	1997	$1,485
4078	IRIS Database-Single User	1997	$495
510	ISO 14000: Understanding Environmental Standards	1996	$69
551	ISO 14001: An Executive Repoert	1996	$55
518	Lead Regulation Handbook	1996	$79
478	Principles of EH&S Management	1995	$69
554	Property Rights: Understanding Government Takings	1997	$79
582	Recycling & Waste Mgmt Guide to the Internet	1997	$49
603	Superfund Manual, 6th Edition	1997	$115
566	TSCA Handbook, 3rd Edition	1997	$95
534	Wetland Mitigation: Mitigation Banking and Other Strategies	1997	$75

PC #	SAFETY AND HEALTH TITLES	Pub Date	Price
547	Construction Safety Handbook	1996	$79
553	Cumulative Trauma Disorders	1997	$59
559	Forklift Safety	1997	$65
539	Fundamentals of Occupational Safety & Health	1996	$49
535	Making Sense of OSHA Compliance	1997	$59
563	Managing Change for Safety and Health Professionals	1997	$59
589	Managing Fatigue in Transportation, ATA Conference	1997	$75
4086	OSHA Technical Manual, Electronic Edition	1997	$99
598	Project Mgmt for E H & S Professionals	1997	$59
552	Safety & Health in Agriculture, Forestry and Fisheries	1997	$125
523	Safety & Health on the Internet	1996	$39
597	Safety Is A People Business	1997	$49
463	Safety Made Easy	1995	$49
590	Your Company Safety and Health Manual	1997	$79

G̣ ORDER FORM

Qty.	Product Code	Title	Price

Subtotal_____

MD Residents add 5% Sales Tax_____

Shipping and Handling_____

Within US: Add $6/item for 1-4 items. Add $3/item for 5+ items/
Outside US. Add $15 /item for Airmail. Add $10/item for Surface

Payment Enclosed_____

Method of Payment

❑ Check (*payable to Government Institutes in US dollars*) $ _____

❑ Purchase Order (please attach to this order form)

❑ Credit Card: Exp.___/____ ❑ MC ❑ VISA ❑ AMEX

Credit Card No. _____

Signature. _____

Name: _____
Company: _____
Address: _____
City:/ _____ State/Province: _____
Zip/Postal Code: _____ Country: _____
Telephone: _____ Fax: _____
E-mail Address: _____

Government Institutes

4 Research Place, Suite 200 • Rockville, MD 20850-3226
Tel. (301) 921-2355 • FAX (301) 921-0373
E-mail: giinfo@govinst.com • Internet: http://www.govinst.com